A GUIDE TO BUILDING GENERATIONAL WEALTH IN EAST AFRICAN FAMILIES

Kakurah Ninsiima

Nove Terra

NoveTerra Publishing

Kakurah D Ninsiima

Disclaimer

This book is intended to provide general financial education and personal development information to individuals and families seeking to build and preserve generational wealth, particularly within East African and diaspora communities. It is not intended as legal, tax, investment, or financial advice. Readers are encouraged to consult qualified professionals for specific advice tailored to their individual circumstances.

While every effort has been made to ensure the accuracy of the information presented, the author and publisher make no representations or warranties regarding the completeness, accuracy, or applicability of any content in this book. The author and publisher disclaim any liability, loss, or risk incurred as a direct or indirect consequence of the use and application of any contents of this book.

All examples, case studies, and stories are for illustrative purposes only. Any resemblance to real persons, living or dead, or real events is purely coincidental unless explicitly stated otherwise.

For permissions, contact:

Nove Terra Publishing
Paperback ISBN: 978-1-0688746-0-4
eBook ISBN: 978-1-0688746-0-4

Published by Nove Terra Publishing
Printed in Canada

Foreword

Building wealth that lasts for generations is not just about making money it's about breaking free from financial struggles, helping families grow, and creating a strong future. Many East African families face economic hardships and cultural challenges that make financial success seem out of reach. But within these communities, there is strength, creativity, and a deep desire to build something better for the future.

In Building Generational Wealth in East African Families: A Practical Guide for Creating Lasting Financial Legacies, Kakurah Ninsiima has written a book that goes beyond basic money lessons. This book is not just about saving and investing it's about changing the way we think about money. It encourages families and communities to take control of their finances and build wealth that will last for many generations.

What makes this book different is that it looks at the big picture. It doesn't just talk about personal finance but also explores topics like starting a business, making smart investments, learning about money, and planning for the future. The author also includes important lessons from traditional East African financial practices, like group savings and community support, and explains how they can be used in today's world to build wealth.

This book is not only for individuals it is also a valuable resource for community leaders, non-profits, and organizations that want to improve financial well-being in their communities. With real-life examples, group activities, and useful tips, this book is a powerful tool for anyone who wants to make a difference. Whether you want to improve your own finances, help your family succeed, or support your community, the knowledge in this book will be helpful to you.

This is more than just another book about money,it is a guide to building a better future. The ideas and lessons here can help not only East Africans but people everywhere. By following the steps in this book, readers will be able to create lasting financial security for themselves and future generations.

Let this book be your guide to financial success. It is time to take action, break old patterns, and build a legacy that will last.

Dr, Bielu, A Onyekwelu.

INTRODUCTION

Have you ever wondered what it takes to break the cycle of financial struggle and build a legacy that lasts for generations? In East Africa, where the dreams of many are often overshadowed by economic challenges, the journey to financial success can feel daunting. Yet, within our communities lie untapped potential, rich traditions, and innovative minds ready to redefine the narrative of wealth.

The Reality of Financial Struggles

Did you know that over **60%** of East African families live paycheck to paycheck, struggling to save for their futures? This statistic isn't just a number; it reflects the hardships of countless individuals. The challenge is not merely about earning a paycheck; it's about transforming that income into lasting wealth. Building generational wealth is not just an ambition; it's a necessity for transforming lives and communities.

The Importance of Generational Wealth

Generational wealth refers to the assets passed down from one generation to another, providing financial security and opportunities for future family members. It encompasses not only financial resources but also knowledge, skills, and values that empower families to thrive. In East Africa, where economic disparities are significant, creating a legacy of wealth can change the trajectory of entire families.

Why This Book?

In "*Building Generational Wealth in East African Families: A Practical Guide for Creating Lasting Financial Legacies*,"

The struggle to break away from familial financial burden from one generation to the other is an African problem and not peculiar to East Africa. While I aim to provide you with practical strategies and insights tailored specifically for the East African context ***the insight and experiences shared in this book certainly would benefit all Africans in general.***

My goal is to empower you with the tools to create a prosperous legacy for your family. Drawing from my personal journey, from living paycheck to paycheck to discovering the transformative power of financial education, I understand the struggles and triumphs of navigating this path.

Let's talk about something real. If you're reading this, you probably want more for yourself and your family. You want to break free from survival mode, build lasting wealth, and create opportunities that stretch beyond just your lifetime. But maybe you're wondering: *Is this book really for me?*

I get it. When people talk about wealth-building, it can sometimes feel like they're speaking to those who already have a financial head start. But let me be clear, this book isn't just for the wealthy or for those who already have disposable income to invest. It's for *anyone* who's ready to shift their mindset and act, no matter where they're starting from.

That being said, I won't sugarcoat reality. If you're in a situation where every dollar is a fight for survival, where putting food on the table is the immediate priority, then some of the strategies in this book may not be immediately actionable. And that's okay. *Knowledge is power.* Even if you're not in a position to save or invest right now, understanding the principles of wealth creation will equip you for when the right moment comes.

This book is for:

✅ The working professional who wants to stop living paycheck to paycheck

✅ The entrepreneur looking for ways to grow and protect their income

✅ The parent who wants to secure a better future for their children

✅ The dreamer who refuses to accept that financial struggle is their only option

✅ The hustler, the builder, the one who's willing to do the work

If any of that sounds like you, then welcome. You're exactly where you need to be.

Key Themes We Will Explore

In the upcoming pages, we'll explore several essential themes that are crucial for creating and sustaining generational wealth:

1. **Entrepreneurship:** We'll discuss strategies for starting and growing businesses in local contexts, highlighting success stories that resonate with East African families.
2. **Investment Strategies:** A few key and easily accessible investments opportunities will be explored including

specific methods for investing in real estate, agriculture, and stocks, with a focus on practical application.

3. **Financial Education:** Practical modules on budgeting, investment simulations, and understanding credit will be provided to improve financial literacy.
4. **Underrepresentation of Informal Economies:** We'll explore how to leverage informal savings groups, such as stokvels, susu, and SACCOs,within formal financial planning.
5. **Risk Management:** Insights on assessing and managing risks, particularly concerning political instability and market fluctuations, will be discussed.
6. **Cultural Barriers:** We will analyze specific cultural beliefs that hinder financial growth and propose actionable strategies to overcome them.
7. **Community Involvement:** The importance of community support and collaborative projects in wealth-building efforts will be emphasized.
8. **Legacy Planning:** A comprehensive section on creating a lasting legacy will include guidance on trust formation, ethical inheritance practices, and estate planning.
9. **Technological Advances:** We will explore how technology, including digital tools and fintech innovations, can aid in wealth creation.
10. **Ongoing Learning Resources:** Finally, I will provide a curated list of resources for continued financial education and community support.

A Transformative Journey

Through engaging stories, expert insights, and actionable steps, this book will guide you on your path to financial success.

Together, we will navigate the unique challenges of our region, tapping into our rich cultural heritage while embracing modern financial practices.

Call to Action

Join me on this transformative journey to elevate your wealth and secure a brighter future for generations to come. As we embark on this exploration, I encourage you to reflect on your financial goals, the legacy you wish to leave, and the practical steps you can take today to start building a more prosperous tomorrow.

1 - Cultivating Business Mindsets in East Africa

Entrepreneurship Begins at Home

In the bustling Kawangware market of Nairobi, Amina's story begins, not with a business plan or bank loan, but with a cooking pot and determination. Having never completed primary school, she couldn't read business books or write the simplest business proposal or plan. But what she possessed was far more valuable: deep knowledge of her community's needs and exceptional cooking skills passed down from her mother.

Starting From What You Have

1. Amina's journey into business wasn't sparked by entrepreneurial ambition but by necessity. When her husband's casual labour jobs became irregular, she began selling mandazi and chai from a small table outside her house. She didn't need market research reports to know her customers, her daily interactions gave her a deep understanding of what people needed, an affordable breakfast. Her first customers were neighbours who could smell her fresh mandazi in the morning.

Understanding Real Risks

Many idealistic organizations encourage taking loans to start businesses. They paint pictures of rapid growth and quick success. But this advice often ignores the harsh realities of small business failures. For entrepreneurs without financial buffers, loans can be a double-edged sword, offering capital but also creating pressure that can backfire. Had Amina followed this path and taken a loan, she would have faced crushing pressure. A few slow weeks, a family emergency, or spoiled ingredients could have left her deeper in poverty, struggling to repay debt while feeding her children. Instead, she chose a strategy of steady, organic growth, minimizing financial risk while maximizing flexibility.

Scaling Without Debt

Instead, Amina chose a different path. Each day, she set aside KSh 50 from her earnings. Some days, she couldn't save anything, but she never went into debt. When customers started asking if she could cook for their small family gatherings, she used her savings to buy a larger pot. Her approach demonstrated a crucial principle: reinvesting profits strategically rather than taking on external risk. She tested new recipes at home, serving them to neighbours for honest feedback before adding them to her offerings. This iterative approach, testing, refining, then expanding, helped her minimize mistakes and meet real demand.

Building Trust Before Growth

Word spread about Amina's cooking, not through marketing plans or social media, but through satisfied customers telling their friends and family. She became known for her reliability and generous portions. Her growing clientele didn't come from expensive advertising,it came from trust. In many informal economies, reputation is a business's strongest currency. Local church groups began requesting her services for their meetings. Some customers couldn't pay immediately, but she knew which ones to trust based on their standing in the community.

Learning Through Experience

While Amina couldn't read business manuals, she developed sharp skills in mental arithmetic. She knew exactly how much she spent on ingredients and how much she needed to charge to make a profit. She learned to estimate the right quantities for events by experience, reducing waste, and maximizing earnings. These practical skills proved more valuable than any theoretical knowledge. In many cases, direct experience is the best business education, especially in environments where formal training is limited.

The Power of Community Networks

As her reputation grew, Amina developed relationships with other market vendors. The vegetable seller would alert her to good deals on tomatoes and onions. The butcher would keep choice cuts for her catering orders. Her network wasn't built through formal business events but through daily interactions, proving that community-driven relationships can be just as valuable as corporate networking.

Managing Money Wisely

Without access to formal banking initially, Amina joined a local women's savings group. Each week, members contributed what they could and took turns receiving the collected sum. This system helped her save for larger purchases without risking loans. When she finally approached a bank years later, she did so from a position of strength, with an established customer base and a proven business model.

Measured Growth for Long-Term Success

Today, Amina's business supports her family and employs three other women from her community. Her growth happened in step with her ability to manage operations effectively, never expanding faster than she could sustain. She still works from home, having converted part of her house into a kitchen rather than renting an expensive commercial space. Each expansion decision is made carefully, based on genuine demand rather than borrowed money.

Understanding Success

Success for Amina isn't measured in profit margins or market share. It's measured in her ability to pay her children's school fees, provide a stable income for her employees, and maintain her reputation in the community. She's living proof that entrepreneurship isn't just about wealth, it's about stability, independence, and long-term impact.

Key Takeaways

True entrepreneurship often looks different from what business books describe. Success comes not from elaborate plans or borrowed money, but from understanding your community, starting with what you have, and growing carefully. The best business advice isn't always found in textbooks - it's found in the practical wisdom of people like Amina who build sustainable businesses through patience, hard work, and deep community connections.

Entrepreneurship is often romanticized,stories of successful business owners who "started from nothing" and built empires inspire many. But the truth? **Success is never a straight line.** It's full of twists, setbacks, and unexpected challenges.

Take Amina's story, for example. She started with nothing but a dream, a few savings, and a small food business. With discipline and persistence, she turned it into a thriving enterprise. **But can everyone replicate her success?** Yes,**but not always in the exact same way.**

The reality is that life happens. A sudden illness in the family, a financial crisis, or unforeseen responsibilities can disrupt even the best-laid plans. Does that mean the dream dies? Not at all. These are **exceptions, not the norm.** The key is **building a mindset of resilience and adaptability.**

Success Beyond a Single Industry

Many people assume that food businesses are the easiest path to financial stability because, after all, everyone needs to eat. While that's true, **there are many other pathways to success.** The most successful entrepreneurs in East Africa are those who look beyond a single market and identify **gaps in foundational community services.**

Consider these areas:

- **Agribusiness & Value Addition** – Processing coffee, honey, and grains for export rather than selling raw products.

- **Education & Skills Training** – Building vocational training centers to equip young people with practical skills.

- **Technology & Digital Services** – Mobile payment solutions, e-commerce, and IT services that bridge the gap in underdeveloped sectors.

- **Healthcare & Wellness** – Affordable community clinics, herbal remedies, and fitness centers.

Resilience: The Mindset That Wins

The difference between those who succeed and those who don't isn't just access to capital,it's **the mindset.** The best entrepreneurs understand that **setbacks are part of the process.** They don't wait for perfect conditions; they take action, learn from failures, and adapt quickly.

So, whether you choose cooking, trade, agriculture, or technology, **the key to success is not just the business you choose,it's the ability to persist, pivot, and persevere.**

Defining Your Purpose

Objective: To set intentions and goals for how you will use the knowledge from this book.

This book is more than just a collection of ideas, it is a roadmap to real change. Your journey toward building generational wealth begins with understanding your "*why*" and establishing a deep sense of purpose. What are you hoping to achieve by reading this book, and how will you apply it to your life?

Exercise 1: Setting Your Intentions

Instructions: Before proceeding further, take a moment to set your intentions for reading this book. What do you hope to achieve? Write down at least 3 goals that you want to accomplish through the knowledge and strategies presented in this book.

Reflection Questions:

1. How will these goals impact your family's financial future?
2. What specific steps can you take to integrate the lessons from this book into your daily life?
3. What challenges might you face as you begin this journey, and how will you overcome them?

Space for Notes:

Exercise 2: Creating Your Financial Action Plan

Instructions: Now that you've set your intentions, it's time to create an action plan. Based on what you've learned so far, write down the immediate actions you will take in the next 30 days to start building wealth.

Reflection Questions:

1. What is the first step you can take today to move toward your generational wealth goals?
2. How will you hold yourself accountable to the action plan you've set?

Space for Notes:

2 - Understanding Investment

Investment might sound like a term for big corporations or city professionals, but in reality, it's a part of our everyday life in our communities. Look around you,the farmer storing grain until prices improve, the shopkeeper stocking up during low seasons, or the parent carefully saving for school fees. These aren't just daily activities; they're investment strategies passed down through generations.

At its core, investment is about making strategic choices today that will yield greater benefits tomorrow, whether in business, relationships, or personal growth. Have you ever wondered what differentiates successful businesspeople in our communities from those who struggle? It's not about making quick money or taking big risks. Instead, it's about understanding the difference between gambling and investing, between chasing quick profits and building something that lasts.

Learning from Our Own

Take James Omondi's story from Kisumu's-Kenya main market. Fifteen years ago, he was just another vegetable seller, but he saw something others missed. "*I noticed that tomato prices would double or triple during certain months*," he tells us with a knowing smile. "*So, I started setting aside KSh 200 each day to buy extra tomatoes when prices were low.*"

James's success wasn't about having lots of money,it was about understanding patterns. "*Some vendors try to sell everything at once*," he explains, gesturing at his now-diverse stall. "*But I learned it's better to know one product deeply before adding another. Each new item was like planting another seed.*"

The Power of Small Steps

Think about building a house. Would you start with the roof? of course not. The same principle applies to investment. Sarah Mugisha from Kampala- Uganda shows us how patience builds prosperity. She began with just one sewing machine, making clothes for neighbour's. While others urged her to take loans and expand quickly, she remembered her friend's business crumbling under debt payments when sales were slow.

"*Everyone wanted me to dream bigger, faster,*" Sarah recalls, now teaching at her own tailoring school. "*But I chose to dream smarter*." She understood that a strong foundation matters more than rapid expansion. Two years of saving led to a second machine. Teaching her sister to sew doubled the production without debt. Today, her school trains new generations of tailors, built on a foundation of patience and careful planning.

Wisdom in Community

Have you ever noticed how our traditional practices often hold more wisdom than modern financial advice? In Moshi, Tanzania, twenty women prove this through their *mkopo* (lending circle). Each week, they contribute TSh 10,000, but money is just the beginning of their investment.

"*When my roof leaked during the rainy season,*" Mama Hadija shares, "*the group helped me repair it before my fabric stock could be damaged. That's an investment too – building relationships that protect your business*." Their success springs from weekly meetings, careful record-keeping, and collective decision-making. Their story reminds us that investment isn't just about money—it's about insight, timing, and relationships.

Planting Trees for Tomorrow

Think of investment like planting a mango tree, it requires patience, care, and faith in the future. Hassan Mohamed in Lamu, a city in Kenya understood this when he started with just one goat, saved from his fishing income. While others chased quick profits, he focused on building his herd slowly and steadily.

"*Many people want quick money,*" he reflects, watching his goats graze, "*but lasting wealth grows slowly, like a baobab tree.*" Today, his herd provides regular income from milk and occasional sales, proving that patient investment bears the sweetest fruit.

The Power of Unity

Sometimes, the best investments are those we make together. In Gulu, Uganda, ten farmers proved this by pooling their resources to buy a grain mill. Each contributed according to their means, from USh 50,000 to USh 200,000, but more importantly, they contributed their trust and commitment.

"*Alone, none of us could afford the mill,*" Grace Akello explains, "*but together, we created something that serves the whole village and earns us all money.*" Their success grew from clear agreements, regular meetings, and shared responsibility,showing how community investment can multiply individual resources.

Learning from Each Step

What if your investment doesn't work out as planned? Mary Kamau's story teaches us that even setbacks carry valuable lessons. After losing money on land with unclear ownership, she turned her experience into wisdom for others. "*That mistake taught me to always verify before investing,*" she shares. "*Now, I help others avoid the same problem.*" Her story is a powerful reminder that lessons learned from failure can be just as valuable as financial gains.

Seeing Beyond the Obvious

What problem in your community could become your opportunity? Agnes Mutua asked herself this question while watching farmers struggle to transport produce to market. Instead of buying new clothes that month, she invested in a *mkokoteni* (handcart). "*Now it earns money every day,*" she says proudly, "*and I'm saving for a second one.*"

But Agnes's real investment wasn't just the cart. She invested time learning farmers' harvest schedules, building relationships, and maintaining her cart meticulously. "*Many people see only the cart,*" she observes, "*but the real investment is in the service and relationships.*" Her story highlights a key lesson: success comes not just from assets, but from how well you use them.

Growing Through Change

How do you protect your future against life's uncertainties? Our communities have developed wisdom for this too. Consider the Maasai practice of keeping different types of livestock in various locations—it's nature's way of teaching us not to put all our eggs in one basket.

John Kiprop from Eldoret, Kenya applies this ancient wisdom to his modern shop. "*I sell vegetables, clothes, and household items,*" he explains. "*When one type of business is slow, the others keep money flowing.*" His careful records of seasonal sales patterns help him invest wisely in stock, showing how traditional wisdom can guide modern success.

Remember, investment isn't about getting rich quickly, it's about growing wealth steadily and safely. Start with what you know well. Save regularly, even if it's small amounts. Learn from your community's experience. Most importantly, treat your investments like a farmer tends crops – with patience, care, and faith that good seeds planted today will yield a bountiful harvest tomorrow.

The Importance of Generational Wealth

Objective: To understand the importance of building wealth that lasts beyond your lifetime and begins with your family.

Generational wealth is wealth that is passed down through generations, wealth that not only benefits you but also your children, grandchildren, and beyond. Building generational wealth is not just about financial prosperity but about instilling values, wisdom, and a legacy that will endure for years to come.

Exercise 3: Defining Your Legacy

Instructions: Reflect on what you want to leave behind for future generations. Write down what you hope your legacy will be. This can include financial assets, but also values, traditions, and life lessons.

Reflection Questions:

1. What is your vision for your family's financial future?
2. What steps can you take today to start creating this legacy?
3. How do you want future generations to remember your contribution to the family's wealth?

Space for Notes:

Exercise 4: Visualizing Generational Wealth

Instructions: Picture what your family will look like in 20, 30, or 50 years. What role will your children and grandchildren play in preserving or growing the wealth you've created?

Reflection Questions:

1. What values will you pass down that will help sustain the wealth you've built?
2. How can you involve your children and family members in your financial journey today?

3. How can your small community business transform into a heritable business for your children and grandchildren?

Space for Notes:

3 - The Art of Money Management

Have you ever watched a skilled weaver at work? Each thread has its place, each pattern its purpose. Money management in our communities works the same way – weaving small, intentional habits that add up to lasting financial security. Some of the most masterful money managers never set foot in a classroom, yet their wisdom often surpasses that of financial experts.

The Market's Money Master

Take a walk through the bustling Kariakoo Market in Dar es Salaam, Tanzania and you might meet Mama Kudi. For twenty years, she has run her vegetable business with the precision of a conductor, despite never learning to read or write. "*Watch this*," she'll tell you with a knowing smile, pulling out different packets from her kanga. "*This pocket is for tomorrow's stock, this one guards school fees, and this small one stands ready for emergencies. Mix everything together, and your money slips away like water through your fingers.*"

What's Mama Hadija's secret? Not formal education – but an unwavering system and iron discipline. Every sunset brings her daily ritual: counting, dividing, and planning. While other vendors struggled during lean seasons, her stall remained stocked. Why? Because she treated business money as sacred, never blending it with personal needs.

"*You know what I see?*" she asks, watching younger vendors count their day's earnings. "*Many earn good money but lose it because they have no system. A system is like a shepherd for your money – it keeps it from wandering away.*"

The Three-Pot Wisdom

Long before banks lined our streets, our ancestors knew the art of money management. In Nakuru, Kenya a Grandmother Wanjiru's three-pot system has guided three generations of her family.
Picture three clay pots: one for daily bread, one for dreams yet to bloom (like school fees), and one for life's surprises. "*Money is like water*," she would say, her eyes twinkling. "*Without proper channels, it flows away before you know it.*"
This wisdom flows like a river through her family. Her daughter Joyce modernized clay pots into paper envelopes, while granddaughter Rebecca uses her hair salon's finances through three mobile money accounts. "*The vessels change*," Rebecca reflects, "*but Grandmother's wisdom remains. Never mix money meant for different purposes*."

The Shopkeeper's Revelation

Every scar teaches a lesson, and Ibrahim's failed shop in Kampala, Uganda taught him plenty. "*I used to treat my shop like a personal wallet,*" he admits, now running a thriving business. "*Business money, household money – everything swirled together until nothing remained.*"
Today, Ibrahim's humble notebook tells his business's story through three daily numbers: money in, stock out, and home expenses. "*These three numbers*," he says, tapping his notebook, "*they're like a doctor's checkup for my business. They tell me if it's healthy or needs care.*"
This simple habit revealed hidden patterns. End-of-month rush? Stock up. Slow school-opening weeks? Save more. Sometimes, the deepest wisdom lies in the smallest observations.

The Power of Together

Walk through Mombasa's in Kenya lively streets, and you might hear about the bodaboda riders who turned daily savings into shared strength. Each day, KSh 200 goes into their shared lockbox – a small amount that grows mighty through consistency and trust. "*Saving alone*?" Hassan, one of the members, shakes his head. "*That's like trying to carry water in one hand. But together? We carry an ocean.*" Their system demands three keys held by different members; monthly openings witnessed by all eyes. From these savings, motorcycles have been bought, medical emergencies covered, and businesses launched.

Planting Money Wisdom in Young Soil

In Rwanda, Kigali's vibrant market, Sarah plants seeds of financial wisdom in her children's minds. Her daughter's fingers dance through daily counts, while her son tracks stock with careful notes. "*They're not just learning numbers,*" Sarah explains, watching them work. "*They're learning that money needs attention, just like our garden at home.*"

Each child tends their own savings tin, even if only 100 francs find their way in. "*Big dreams grow from small seeds,*" Sarah tells them, sharing stories of her own journey from selling eggs to running her vegetable stand. Her daughter's chickens now lay golden eggs of their own, while her son saves half of every gift – tomorrow's business leaders growing strong roots today.

Dancing with Uncertainty

Think of Mutesi, a farmer nurturing Rwanda's rich soil, dividing her harvest earnings like a master chef: one portion for today's meal, one for tomorrow's seeds, and one for life's surprises.

"*Eating all your harvest at once?*" she asks with gentle wisdom. "*That's like trying to feed yourself for a year with one meal.*" When heavy rains tested her community, Mutesi's foresight proved golden. While others sought costly loans, her emergency savings carried her family through. "*They called me too careful,*" she recalls with quiet pride. "*But in farming and in money, careful hands harvest the sweetest fruits.*"

Building Your Money Wisdom

Now, let's turn these stories into action. Take a moment to consider:
What's your current money system? Is it serving you like Mama Hadija's pockets, or letting your money slip away?
How could you create your own three-pot system using what you have, be it envelopes, mobile money, or actual containers?
Who could be your saving partners, like the bodaboda riders of Mombasa?
Remember, these practices aren't just African wisdom. they echo financial truths recognized worldwide. From the market stalls of Dar es Salaam to the banking halls of New York, the principles remain: separate, save, plan, and grow together.

Key Principles for Your Journey

- **Create Clear Channels:** Like Mama Hadija's pockets, give every shilling its purpose.
- **Build Your Safety Net:** Whether it's Grandmother Wanjiru's emergency pot or Mutesi's harvest division, save for tomorrow's surprises.
- **Find Your Tribe:** Like the bodaboda riders, join hands with others to make saving easier and more accountable.

- **Teach and Learn:** Share wisdom as Sarah does with her children, growing money knowledge across generations.
- **Start Small, Stay Consistent:** Remember Ibrahim's three daily numbers ,sometimes the simplest systems work best.
- Discipline and prudent expenditure plans cannot be overemphasized. Avoid partying today, rather save to party harder tomorrow!

Your journey to better money management starts with a single step. Like the market vendors, shopkeepers, and farmers in our stories, you don't need complex education or huge amounts to begin. You just need to start, stay consistent, and let your system grow strong like a baobab tree, one day at a time.
What will be your first step today?

The Reality of Financial Struggles

Objective: To assess your current financial situation and gain clarity about your financial challenges.

Before embarking on the journey of building generational wealth, it's crucial to understand where you currently stand. Financial struggles are common, but they can be overcome with the right mindset, tools, and strategies. In this exercise, we will help you assess your financial situation and identify the obstacles that are holding you back.

Exercise 5: Mapping Your Financial Landscape

Instructions: Take a moment to honestly assess your current financial situation. Write down all of the financial struggles you are experiencing. Be specific, think about both short-term and long-term challenges.

- **Short-Term Challenges**: What are the immediate financial issues you face? (e.g., debt, lack of savings, job insecurity)
- **Long-Term Challenges**: What financial obstacles could potentially affect your future? (e.g., no investments, poor credit score, lack of retirement savings) inappropriate spending patterns, financial imprudence, etc.

Reflection Questions:

1. What are the primary obstacles preventing your financial progress?
2. How do these obstacles make you feel? What emotions are attached to your financial struggles?
3. What immediate steps can you take to begin overcoming these obstacles?

Space for Notes:

Exercise 6: Identifying Your Financial Priorities

Instructions: Reflect on what matters most to you in terms of financial security. This can include the health and well-being of your family, buying a home, building a business, or planning for retirement.

Write down your top 3 financial priorities. These are the goals you want to focus on in the next 1-3 years.

Reflection Questions:

1. Why are these financial priorities important to you?
2. How do your financial struggles impact these priorities?
3. What can you do today to start aligning your actions with your financial priorities?

Space for Notes:

Activity

Write down your monthly income and divide it into categories like Mama Hadija or Joyce. Reflect on how this practice could improve your financial discipline.

4 - Understanding Entrepreneurship

Building Your Dream: A Guide to Local Entrepreneurship

Have you ever watched a seed grow into a mighty tree? Starting a business in East Africa is much the same. beginning small, requiring patience, and with the right care, growing into something that provides shade and sustenance for generations. Every day across our region, ordinary people are planting these seeds of enterprise, nurturing them with determination and wisdom passed down through generations.

The Spark of Possibility

Picture yourself walking through any marketplace in East Africa. Listen to the rhythm of commerce, the friendly bargaining, the cheerful greetings, the steady hum of countless small businesses working together. This is where dreams take root and grow into reality.

Take Aisha Kimani's story. Not long ago, she stood on her family's three-acre farm in rural Kenya, watching her parents struggle with traditional farming methods that barely fed the family. Many would have accepted this as their fate, but not Aisha. When she heard about a local agricultural training program, she saw her chance.

"*Everyone thought I was crazy to try new farming methods,*" she recalls with a laugh. "*But I could see the possibility of something better.*" Within eighteen months of implementing organic farming techniques, Aisha transformed that struggling farm into a thriving enterprise that now supplies fresh produce to three major restaurants in Nakuru, Kenya and employs six community members.

Planting Your Business Seed

But how do you start? Where do you find your own spark of possibility? Let's break it down into manageable steps:

First: Listen and Learn

Before you plant a seed, you study the soil. Before starting a business, study your community:

- What problems do people complain about?
- What services do they travel far to find?
- What traditional solutions could be improved?

The Karanja family in Nairobi found their opportunity by listening carefully. "*We noticed young professionals talking about wanting traditional medicines, but in a modern, reliable form*," explains Mrs. Karanja. "*Our grandmother's herbal knowledge was the key – we just needed to package it for today's market*."

Second: Plan Your Garden

Just as a farmer plans their fields, you need to plan your business:

- Map out your startup costs.
- Identify your target customers.
- List potential challenges.
- Plan how you'll handle seasonal changes.

"*I spent three months planning before I sold my first herb mixture*," Mrs. Karanja shares. "*People called it wasted time, but that planning saved us when challenges came.*"

Third: Finding Water for Your Seeds

Money is like water for your business, you need it to grow. But here's the secret many successful East African entrepreneurs know: banks aren't the only source. Consider:

- Joining a SACCO (Savings and Credit Cooperative)
- Creating a small investment group with trusted friends
- Exploring microfinance options
- Investigating government and NGO programs for small businesses

The Abdi brothers in Uganda started their phone repair shop with money from their family investment group. "*Each week, ten family members contributed what they could*," Mohammed Abdi explains. "*Some weeks it was only 5,000 shillings, but it grew steadily like a termite hill.*"

Fourth: Facing the Storms

Every business faces challenges. Let's be honest about them:

Infrastructure Challenges

- Unreliable electricity? Keep manual records as a backup.
- Poor roads? Build delivery time buffers into your promises.
- Limited internet? Download essential information during good connection times.

Market Challenges

- Seasonal changes in customer spending
- New competitors entering your market
- Changes in supply costs

Personal Challenges

- Balancing family and business demands
- Managing stress during difficult times
- Maintaining motivation when growth is slow

"*The secret,*" says Aisha, "*is to expect challenges and prepare for them. I keep three months of savings just for hard times. When others panic during dry seasons, I stay calm.*"

Growing Strong Roots

Your business needs strong roots to survive storms. Here's how to build them:

Community Connections

- Join local business associations.
- Find a mentor who's succeeded in your field.
- Build relationships with other entrepreneurs.
- Support your community through your business.

Smart Technology Use

Start simple and grow gradually:

- Begin with basic phone-based record keeping.
- Use mobile money services.

- Gradually add digital tools as needed.
- Always keep paper backups.

Customer Care

- Know your customers by name.
- Remember their preferences.
- Ask for feedback regularly.
- Solve problems quickly.

Remember this: **every successful business you see started with someone like you** – someone who saw a possibility and dared to try. The Karanjas didn't know their traditional medicine business would succeed. Aisha couldn't be certain her organic farming would work. The Abdi brothers weren't sure their phone repair shop would grow.

But they all shared one thing: they started. They took that first step, then another, then another.

Your Next Steps

1. **This week:** Write down three problems you see in your community that could be business opportunities.
2. **Next week:** Talk to five potential customers about these problems.
3. **Within a month:** Create a basic plan for your chosen business idea.
4. **Within two months:** Identify possible funding sources
5. **Within three months:** Take your first small step into business.

Start Small, Start Smart

Remember: **You don't need to start big**. Start small but start smart. Learn from those around you. Use both traditional wisdom and modern knowledge. Most importantly, begin your journey now.

What problem in your community could become your opportunity? What first step will you take today?

Your business journey isn't just about making money, it's about creating something valuable for your community, something that could last for generations. Like a baobab tree, it starts as a tiny seed but has the potential to grow into something magnificent that provides shade and sustenance for many.

The Power of Entrepreneurship

Objective: To understand the crucial role entrepreneurship plays in wealth-building and to explore how to harness the entrepreneurial spirit for financial success.

Entrepreneurship is a key driver of financial independence and long-term prosperity. It empowers individuals to turn ideas into opportunities, solve real-world problems, and create value. Now, take a moment to reflect on your own strengths, interests, and experiences to identify potential business opportunities that align with your unique skills.

Exercise 7: Identifying Your Entrepreneurial Strengths

Instructions: Reflect on your strengths and areas of interest. Think about your skills, experiences, and passions. This exercise will help you identify potential entrepreneurial opportunities that align with your abilities and interests.

Reflection Questions:

1. What skills or talents do you have that could be used to create a business?
2. What industries or fields are you passionate about? How could you translate that passion into a business opportunity?
3. How can you leverage your unique background, experience, or culture to build a successful venture?

Space for Notes:

Exercise 8: Brainstorming Business Ideas

Instructions: Start by brainstorming at least 5 business ideas. These can range from small side projects to larger ventures. The key is to think creatively about what problems you can solve or what needs your community has. Don't censor yourself, let the ideas flow!

Reflection Questions:

1. What are the common problems or unmet needs in your community or industry?
2. How can you tailor a business idea to solve these problems or address these needs?
3. Which of these ideas excites you the most, and why?

Space for Notes:

Exercise 9: Assessing Market Demand

Instructions: Once you've identified a business idea, it's time to assess whether there is market demand. Research local trends, competitors, and consumer behavior to understand the potential for your business idea.

Reflection Questions:

1. What is the current demand for the product or service you're considering?
2. Who are your competitors, and what can you learn from them?
3. What unique value can your business offer that others don't?

Space for Notes:

5 – Building Wealth through Smart Choices

Growing Wealth Through Strategic Investment

Picture a mighty baobab tree. It begins as a tiny seed, much like your savings, but with proper nurturing and time, it grows into something magnificent that can sustain generations. While saving money plants the seed, strategic investment nurtures it into a thriving legacy, providing shelter and security for your family for years to come.

The Bridge from Saving to Investing

Remember Mama Hadija's careful system of separating money into different pockets? Investment takes that wisdom a step further. Instead of just protecting your money, you're putting it to work, whether through property, farmland, or company shares. Each shilling becomes a tiny seed that, when planted wisely, can grow into substantial wealth.

Building on Solid Ground: Real Estate Investment

Walk through any growing East African town, and you'll see the evidence of wise property investment. The Mwanga family's story in Tanzania illustrates what's possible when you combine patience with strategic thinking.

"*Everyone told us we were crazy to buy land so far from town,*" Rebecca Mwanga recalls, laughing. "*But we saw the new road being built, saw young families looking for homes.*" Their journey began with a single plot in what was then a quiet suburb. Instead of rushing to build their dream home, they constructed simple rental units first.

"*Each month's rent went straight into buying materials for the next unit,*" she explains. Within five years, their initial 15-million-shilling investment had grown into a 100-million-shilling property portfolio. Today, their children's education is secured through rental income, and they're helping other families find affordable housing.

Want to follow their path? Consider these proven strategies:

- **Start where you know:** Look for opportunities in neighbourhoods you understand.
- **Follow the signs of growth:** New roads, schools, or markets often signal rising property values.
- **Build-in stages:** Begin with one unit and let it fund the next.
- **Remember location's power:** A small shop in a busy area often outperforms a large building in a quiet zone.

Farming for the Future

Our ancestors knew that land never goes hungry. Today, agricultural investment combines this traditional wisdom with modern market opportunities. Meet the Kamau family, whose coffee farm story might reshape how you view farming as an investment.

"*We started with just two acres and a lot of questions,*" John Kamau shares. "*But we knew coffee was in our blood – my grandfather was a coffee farmer, and global demand keeps growing.*" By reinvesting their profits and applying both traditional knowledge and modern techniques, they expanded to ten acres in just three years.

Consider these agricultural pathways:

- **Cash crops with staying power:** Coffee, tea, macadamia nuts – crops with strong global demand.
- **Value addition:** Instead of just growing, process your harvest to capture more profit.
- **Modern meets traditional:** Use technology to enhance, not replace, proven farming methods.

The beauty of agricultural investment? "*Even in bad years, you can feed your family*," John notes. "*In good years, you can feed your dreams*."

Dancing with the Stock Market

Does the thought of buying company shares make you nervous? You're not alone. But let's learn from the Njeri family in Uganda, who turned their market fears into financial freedom.

"*We started by investing in companies we knew – the businesses whose products we used every day*," Sarah Njeri explains. Their initial 5-million-shilling investment in local blue-chip companies has grown to 20 million shillings through patient investing and dividend reinvestment.

Their advice for stock market success?

- **Start with what you know:** Invest in businesses you understand.
- **Let time be your friend:** Think in years, not months.
- **Spread your risks:** Don't put all your money in one company.
- **Reinvest dividends:** Let your earnings earn more.

Technology and Innovation Investment

The region's burgeoning tech sector presents exciting investment opportunities. When Sarah Ouma invested in a Kenyan health-tech startup, she not only saw her investment triple in value but also contributed to improving healthcare access in her community. Technology investments require careful due diligence but can offer both financial returns and social impact.

Leveraging Community Investment Models

Traditional community investment models like SACCOs and investment clubs continue to play vital roles in wealth building. The Arusha Women's Investment Club demonstrates the power of collective investing. By pooling resources and sharing knowledge, their 50 members have built a diverse investment portfolio spanning real estate, agriculture, and small business ventures. Their success proves that community-based investment models can achieve significant returns while maintaining social bonds.

Diversification

The Makena family's investment journey teaches valuable lessons about risk management. They allocated their investments strategically across real estate (40%), agriculture (30%), stocks (20%), and small business ventures (10%). This diversification helped them weather market fluctuations and generate consistent returns. When their agricultural investments faced challenges during a drought, their rental income provided stability.

Building a Legacy Through Investment

Investment success in East Africa requires balancing immediate returns with long-term wealth building. The Omar family in Tanzania exemplifies this approach. They established a family trust that manages their investments, ensuring wealth preservation and orderly transfer between generations. Their investment decisions consider both financial returns and social impact, creating a legacy that benefits both family and community.

Technology's Role in Modern Investment

Digital platforms have democratized investment access in East Africa. Mobile apps now allow investors to buy stocks, manage real estate, and participate in agricultural investments from their phones. The key lies in combining these modern tools with traditional wisdom. Successful investors often use technology to research opportunities and manage portfolios while maintaining strong personal networks and community connections.

Tools of Modern Investment

Just as mobile money transformed how we handle cash, new digital tools are making investment more accessible. Today, you can check stock prices, manage rental payments, or monitor crop prices – all from your phone. But remember: **technology should enhance, not replace, careful research and wise counsel.**

Building Your Investment Community

No mighty tree grows alone – it needs the right environment to thrive. The same is true for your investments. Joining an investment group fosters shared knowledge and collective growth.

The Nairobi Investment Club shows the power of community – their members achieve average returns of 15% annually by sharing insights and combining resources for bigger opportunities.

Protecting Your Investment Garden

Every garden needs protection from storms. Here's how successful investors guard their wealth:

- **Never invest everything:** Keep emergency funds separate.
- **Start small, learn big:** Begin with what you understand, then expand.
- **Seek wise counsel:** Learn from those who've succeeded.
- **Keep clear records:** Track every shilling invested and returned.

Remember, **every successful investor started exactly where you are today**. The Mwanga family didn't begin with a property empire. The Kamaus started with just two acres. The Njeris began with shares in companies they knew well.

Your next steps:

1. **Look around your community:** What investment opportunities do you see?
2. **Start learning:** What successful investors can you learn from?
3. **Begin small:** What's the smallest investment you could make today?
4. **Build your network:** Who could join your investment journey?

Key takeaways

Investment success in East Africa requires patience, strategic thinking, and cultural awareness. Whether through real estate, agriculture, stocks, or business ventures, the goal remains the same: building sustainable wealth that benefits both family and community. By starting with thorough research, seeking professional guidance when needed, and maintaining a long-term perspective, East African families can create investment portfolios that generate lasting prosperity.

Your investment journey isn't just about growing money – it's about creating opportunities, security, and hope for generations to come. Like our ancestors who planted mango trees knowing their grandchildren would enjoy the fruit, wise investment plants a seed of prosperity that will nourish your family long into the future.

What will be your first step toward growing lasting wealth?

Understanding Investment Basics

Objective: To lay a solid foundation for understanding different types of investments and how they fit into the broader wealth-building strategy.

Smart investing is a key driver of financial growth. From real estate and stocks to bonds and other assets, each investment type comes with its own risks and rewards. Gaining a clear understanding of these options will help you make informed decisions and build a strong financial future. Now, take a moment to assess your current investment knowledge and identify areas for growth.

Exercise 10: Assessing Your Investment Knowledge

Instructions: Evaluate your current understanding of investments. This will help you understand your starting point and areas where you need further education.

Reflection Questions:

1. How familiar are you with different types of investments (real estate, stocks, bonds, etc.)?
2. What types of investments have you considered in the past, and why did you or did you not pursue them?
3. What fears or uncertainties do you have when it comes to investing?

Space for Notes:

Exercise 11: Defining Your Investment Goals

Instructions: Define clear investment goals. Do you want to grow your wealth for retirement? Are you interested in buying property or starting an investment portfolio? Set both short-term and long-term investment goals.

Reflection Questions:

1. What are your financial goals in terms of investing?
2. Are you investing for the long term or looking for quicker returns?
3. How much risk are you willing to take with your investments?

Space for Notes:

Exercise 12: Risk Tolerance Assessment

Instructions: Assess your risk tolerance. Understanding how much risk you are comfortable with is essential for creating an investment strategy. This exercise will help you evaluate your personal risk threshold.

Reflection Questions:

1. How comfortable are you with the possibility of losing money on an investment?
2. What factors influence your decisions when it comes to taking financial risks?
3. How do you plan to manage risk in your investments (e.g., through diversification, insurance, etc.)?

Space for Notes:

6 - Understanding Financial Education

The Power of Financial Education: Your Key to Investment Success

Remember how we talked about investment being like planting a tree? Well, financial education is like learning to be a master gardener. Before you can grow a forest of wealth through investing, you need to understand the soil, the seasons, and the seeds of financial wisdom. While **63%** of East African adults have embraced mobile money services, only **27%** truly understand how to make their money grow. Let's bridge that gap together.

From Knowledge to Power

Think about driving a car - would you get behind the wheel of a car without learning how it works? Similarly, managing money requires understanding its mechanics. This is especially true in East Africa's dynamic economy, where traditional wisdom meets modern financial tools.

Learning from Success: The Abdi Family's Journey

Meet the Abdi family from Somalia. Six months ago, they were like many families - working hard but watching their money slip away like water through their fingers. "*We thought we couldn't save more*," recalls Mama Abdi. "*But then we started tracking every shilling.*"

Their simple act of recording expenses led to an amazing transformation. Their monthly savings jumped from 50,000 to 200,000 Somali shillings. "*Once we saw where our money was going,*" she explains, "*we could direct it where we wanted it, to grow.*" Today, they're not just saving, they're starting to invest in small livestock, their first step toward building real wealth.

Building Your Financial Foundation

Want to follow the Abdi family's path? Here's how to create a budget that works in our unique context:

Map Your Money Rivers

- List all **income sources**, including seasonal changes.
- Track family **support networks**.
- Note **informal business revenue**.
- Remember **agricultural income cycles**.

Watch Your Money Flows

- Use both **digital and paper records**.
- Review **mobile money statements**.
- Keep **receipts for cash transactions**.
- Note **patterns in your spending**.

Honor Your Roots

- Plan for **family obligations**.
- Budget for **community contributions**.
- Set aside funds for **traditional ceremonies**.
- Remember that **cultural investments build social capital**.

Prepare for Storms

- Build an **emergency fund** covering 3-6 months.
- Start **small but be consistent**.
- Keep these funds **separate from investments**.
- Think of it as your **financial umbrella**.

Riding the Digital Wave

East Africa leads the world in mobile money innovation - we process over $40 billion annually through platforms like M-PESA. The Lema family in Tanzania shows us how to surf this digital wave skilfully.

"*At first, we just used M-PESA for basic transfers*," says Mr. Lema, standing in his thriving corner shop. "*Now, it's our business command center*." Their methods?

Smart Mobile Money Management

- Create **separate wallets** for different purposes.
- Set up **automatic savings transfers**.
- Keep detailed **digital records**.
- **Minimize transaction fees** through careful planning.

Bridging Old and New

Connect **mobile money to bank** accounts.

- Explore **digital lending** carefully.
- Consider **micro-insurance** for protection.

- Use **digital payments** to grow your business.

Building Trust: The Credit Journey

In our communities, credit flows through both formal and informal channels, like a river with many streams. The Chanda family's story shows us how to navigate both waters:

Formal Credit Building

- Maintain **regular bank activity**.
- **Contribute to SACCOs** consistently.
- Build a **strong mobile money history.**
- Keep **formal lending records.**

Community Credit Nurturing

- Participate in **lending groups**.
- Build **trust networks**.
- Maintain **perfect repayment records**.
- Gradually **bridge to formal banking**.

Learning by Doing

Would you learn to swim by reading a book? Financial skills grow through practice. Join or start an investment club where you can:

Practice Safely

- Start with **virtual trading accounts**.
- **Analyze markets** together.
- **Track performance** as a group.
- Learn from **shared experiences**.

Step Into Real Markets

- Make **small initial investments**.
- Find **mentors for guidance**.
- **Review results** regularly.
- **Build your portfolio** gradually.

Growing Together: Community Learning

In Rwanda's village savings groups, we see the power of learning together. Like a traditional work party that makes light work of a heavy harvest, collective financial learning multiplies everyone's wisdom.

Learning Activities

- Join **weekly financial discussions**.
- Practice **money management** together.
- Share **success stories**.
- **Support** each other's growth.

Building Support Systems

- Create **savings groups**.
- Explore **joint investments**.
- Start **shared business ventures**.
- Hold each other **accountable**.

Teaching the Next Generation

The Mutua family's Sunday financial review shows us how to pass on financial wisdom:

Family Money Traditions

- Hold weekly **money discussions**.
- Set **monthly goals** together.
- **Plan for the future** as a family.
- **Celebrate** financial victories.

Growing Money Wisdom

- Give **age-appropriate money lessons**.
- Practice **budgeting** together.
- Introduce **investment** concepts early.
- Build **responsible money habits**.

Measuring Your Progress

Like a farmer checking his crops, regular assessment helps your financial education grow:

Track Your Growth

- **Monitor savings** increases.
- Review **investment returns**.
- Watch **debt decrease**.
- See your **wealth grow**.

Plan Your Future

- Set **1-2** year goals.
- Create **3-5** year plans.
- Dream **5+** years ahead.
- **Build your legacy**.

Remember, "*Elimu ni mali*" - education is wealth. Start your financial education journey today:

1. Begin tracking your expenses this week
2. Join a local savings group this month
3. Start your family's money discussions this Sunday
4. Set your first financial goal today

Like a journey of a thousand miles, financial wisdom begins with a single step. What will yours be?

Remember: **Every financially educated family becomes a light for others, illuminating the path to community prosperity**. Your learning journey isn't just about personal growth - it's about lifting up the next generation.

Financial Education: Empowering Yourself and Your Family

Objective: To demonstrate how financial education can be a tool for personal empowerment and how families can work together to build wealth through financial literacy.

Financial knowledge is a powerful tool that benefits individuals and families alike. By fostering financial literacy, setting shared goals, and making informed decisions, families can create a strong foundation for long-term financial success. Now, take the opportunity to develop a family financial education plan that aligns everyone toward common objectives and a secure future.

Exercise 13: Creating a Family Financial Education Plan

Instructions: The best way to ensure long-term financial success is to engage your entire family in wealth-building efforts. Sit down with family members to discuss your collective financial goals and create a shared education plan. This will align everyone toward common objectives and foster a culture of financial literacy within your family.

Reflection Questions:

1. What are your family's current financial strengths and weaknesses?
2. How can you create a family budget that reflects the priorities of all members?
3. What financial skills (e.g., budgeting, saving, investing) does each family member need to improve?

Space for Notes:

Exercise 14: Organizing a Family Financial Workshop

Instructions: Organizing a family financial workshop is a great way to educate everyone on important concepts such as budgeting, saving, and investing. You can either host an in-person meeting or set up a virtual session to discuss financial strategies. In this exercise, we'll map out the structure of a successful family financial workshop.

Reflection Questions:

1. What topics would you want to cover in a family financial workshop (e.g., budgeting, debt management, investment)?
2. How can you ensure that each family member has a chance to participate and share their thoughts?
3. What resources (books, videos, online courses) could you use to facilitate the workshop?

Space for Notes:

Exercise 15: Developing a Personal Financial Education Schedule

Instructions: Continuous learning is essential for improving financial literacy. Create a personal financial education schedule that includes reading books, taking online courses, attending workshops, and learning from mentors.

Reflection Questions:

1. How much time can you realistically dedicate each week to learning about financial matters?
2. What types of resources (books, online courses, podcasts) will you use to improve your financial literacy?
3. How will you hold yourself accountable for your learning progress?

Space for Notes:

7 – Entrepreneurship as a Catalyst for Wealth Creation

In the heart of East Africa's economic renaissance, a powerful transformation is underway. Entrepreneurs are not just building businesses, they're reshaping the region's economic landscape. With over **60%** of the population under 30, East Africa stands at a crucial intersection where youth, technology, and tradition intersect, creating unprecedented opportunities for wealth creation.

The New Face of East African Entrepreneurship

Sarah Mutesi's journey from her grandmother's kitchen in Rwanda to running a regional food processing enterprise captures the essence of modern East African entrepreneurship. "*I didn't just want to preserve our traditional recipes,*" Sarah reflects, "*I wanted to show the world that African cuisine could compete in the global marketplace.*" Her company's growth from a home-based operation to a facility employing 25 people shows the region's broader economic transformation, where traditional practices meet modern business innovation.

Navigating Market Dynamics and Infrastructure Challenges

The path to entrepreneurial success in East Africa requires more than just a good idea, it demands resilience and adaptability. James Ochieng's wellness company in Kenya emerged from a deep understanding of both market gaps and infrastructure limitations. "*When we started, unreliable power supply was our biggest challenge,*" James shares. "*We had to invest in solar backup systems, which ultimately became a competitive advantage.*" His experience highlights how regional challenges can drive innovative solutions.

The Digital Revolution and Traditional Commerce

East Africa's technological leap forward is creating unique opportunities for entrepreneurs. In Uganda, Malik Ibrahim's evolution from mobile phone repair to digital skills education reflects the region's growing tech ecosystem. "*We're not just fixing phones anymore*," Malik explains. "*We're building the next generation of tech entrepreneurs*." This transformation aligns with broader regional trends, where mobile money solutions like M-PESA, MTN & AIRTEL have revolutionized financial access and created new business possibilities.

Capital Access and Creative Financing

The Kagume Sisters' fashion business success in Rwanda demonstrates innovative approaches to funding challenges. Starting with personal savings of 2 million Rwandan francs, they developed a unique rotating credit system with other local entrepreneurs. "*Traditional banks weren't ready to support us,*" explains Marie Kagume. "*So, we created our own funding network*." Their approach represents a growing trend of collaborative financing solutions in response to limited formal lending options.

Climate Change and Business Adaptation

Rebecca Mwangi's pivot from traditional agricultural supplies to climate-smart farming solutions in Kenya exemplifies how environmental challenges are reshaping business opportunities. "*Climate change isn't just a threat—it's creating new markets*," Rebecca notes. Her success in drought-resistant farming techniques has attracted international partnerships, highlighting how local solutions can address global challenges.

The Power of Community and Collective Growth

The Arusha Women's Cooperative's transformation from a small market stall to an international supplier demonstrates the strength of community-based entrepreneurship. Their model of shared resources and knowledge has become a blueprint for similar initiatives across the region, showing how traditional African concepts of *ubuntu* (communal harmony) can create modern business success.

Infrastructure and Scaling Strategies

The Abdalli Brothers' transportation business in Ethiopia provides valuable lessons in scaling within infrastructure constraints. Their systematic approach to fleet expansion, adding vehicles only after achieving 85% utilization, demonstrates how successful entrepreneurs adapt growth strategies to local conditions. "*In East Africa, smart growth often means slow growth,*" explains Ibrahim Abdalli.

Technology as a Growth Catalyst

The region's emerging tech hubs are fostering a new breed of digital entrepreneurs. From fintech startups in Nairobi-Kenya to e-commerce platforms in Kampala-Uganda, technology is enabling businesses to leapfrog traditional development stages. The success of local ride-hailing apps and digital payment solutions shows how technology can address uniquely African challenges while creating scalable businesses.

Future Horizons and Emerging Opportunities

As East Africa continues its economic transformation, new frontiers are opening for entrepreneurs. Renewable energy, educational technology, and sustainable agriculture represent particularly promising sectors. The region's growing middle class, increasing digital connectivity, and young, innovative workforce create perfect conditions for entrepreneurial success.

Key Takeaways

Success in East African entrepreneurship requires a delicate balance of innovation and tradition, technology and human connection, individual initiative, and community support. Whether launching a tech startup in Nairobi-Kenya or a traditional craft business in Zanzibar, entrepreneurs must understand both local realities and global opportunities. The future belongs to those who can navigate these dynamics while creating sustainable value for their communities and the broader region.

The entrepreneurial landscape in East Africa isn't just about individual success stories, it's about building a new economic future. By understanding market needs, embracing technology, adapting to environmental challenges, and maintaining strong community connections, entrepreneurs are creating businesses that will shape the region for generations to come.

Identifying Business Opportunities

Exercise 16: Identifying Local Business Opportunities

Instructions: Think about the unique challenges and opportunities within your local community or country. What industries are underserved? What products or services are in demand? Consider both traditional sectors (like agriculture or retail) and modern industries (like technology and e-commerce).

Reflection Questions:

1. What are the most pressing needs or problems in your local community?
2. How could you address these needs with a new product or service?
3. What opportunities exist in the informal sector that you could tap into?

Space for Notes:

Exercise 17: Navigating Local Business Challenges

Instructions: Entrepreneurship in East Africa often requires creative problem-solving and resilience. Write down any challenges you anticipate in your entrepreneurial journey and think about potential solutions.

Reflection Questions:

1. What are the biggest challenges you expect to face when starting your business?
2. How can you prepare to overcome these challenges (e.g., building a support network, and securing funding)?
3. What resources or mentors can help you navigate the entrepreneurial landscape?

Space for Notes:

8 - Entrepreneurship Strategies

The Entrepreneurial Spirit: Building Tomorrow's Businesses Today

From the buzzing streets of Nairobi-Kenya to the humming tech hubs of Kigali-Rwanda, you'll feel it, the pulse of entrepreneurial energy. In a region where over **60%** of our population is youthful and **85%** of us carry the power of mobile technology in our pockets, opportunities bloom like flowers after the rain. But here's the truth: success requires more than just a brilliant idea. It demands insight to read the market, empathy to understand the community, and patience to build step by step.

The Seeds of Success

Peter Otieno's Journey

Let me share a story that might change how you think about starting a business. Five years ago, Peter Otieno stood on his two acres of land in Kenya, dreaming of something different. While others saw *just* soil and crops, Peter saw a *future* in chemical-free farming. But here's what makes his story special – he didn't rush to plant his first seed.

"*Everyone told me I was wasting time,*" Peter recalls with a smile, "*but I spent my first three months just talking to restaurant owners, understanding their needs.*" This patience paid off. Today, his company, Organic East, has transformed his initial 500,000-shilling investment into a 15-million-shilling enterprise employing 30 community members.

What can we learn from Peter's approach?

- Start with **deep market research**.
- **Build relationships** before seeking sales.
- **Solve real problems** for specific customers.
- **Grow gradually** but **think big**.

The Art of Starting Smart

Binti Fashion's Blueprint

Remember the old saying about measuring twice and cutting once? The founders of Binti Fashion in Rwanda took this wisdom to heart. Before stitching their first design, they spent three months weaving together market research and customer insights.

"*We could have rushed to start production,*" explains Faith, one of the founders. "*Instead, we interviewed working women, studied our competitors, and tested different designs.*" Their patience revealed a hidden opportunity,modern professional women seeking traditional-inspired office wear. By launch day, they had enough pre-orders to cover their initial costs.

This "measure twice, cut once" approach reflects what business experts call the lean startup methodology:

1. **Research your market** deeply.
2. **Test your ideas** with real customers.
3. Adjust based on **feedback**.
4. **Start small but scale smart**.

Finding Your First Shillings

Sarah Mugisha's Smart Start

Money often feels like the biggest mountain to climb when starting a business. But Sarah Mugisha's tech consultancy story shows us a clever path up that mountain. Starting with just 1.2 million Ugandan shillings, combined from personal savings and a SACCO loan – she built her business like a careful farmer tends their crops.

"*I kept my day job for six months*," Sarah shares. "*Every shilling of profit went back into the business.*" Within two years, her company's revenue exceeded her former salary. Her approach teaches us valuable lessons about bootstrap financing:

- **Start** with what you have.
- **Keep your day** job initially if possible.
- **Reinvest** profits consistently.
- **Grow** organically through customer revenue.

Incorporating Technology

The Mwanga Family's Evolution

Think technology is just for big businesses? The Mwanga family's bakery in Tanzania proves otherwise. Their digital journey started with a simple step, accepting mobile money payments. Then came WhatsApp orders. Finally, a basic website for corporate clients. Each step followed customer needs, not just technology trends.

"*We didn't try to do everything at once*," explains Mrs. Mwanga. "*Each digital tool had to make sense for our customers.*" Their gradual approach tripled daily orders while maintaining the personal touch their customers loved.

Turning Challenges into Gold

Hassan Omar's Story

When big electronics stores threatened Hassan Omar's repair shop in Mombasa- Kenya, he didn't panic , he pivoted. His journey from general repairs to high-end smartphone specialist shows us how to turn threats into opportunities.

"*I studied what the big stores weren't doing well,*" Hassan explains. "*They could sell phones, but complex repairs? That became my specialty.*" He invested in specialized tools and training, building expertise the big stores couldn't match.

Hassan's success came from:

- Identifying an underserved niche
- Investing in specialized skills
- Building a reputation for expertise
- Marketing through satisfied customers

The Power of Together

Arusha Women's Business Network

No tree grows strong alone , it needs a forest. The Arusha-Tanzania Women's Business Network proves this business truth. From five women sharing advice over coffee, it has grown into a 200-member force of business transformation.

Members report a **40%** average revenue increase after joining. Why? Because they share more than just business tips, they share dreams, challenges, and solutions. They've created what business experts call a "*knowledge ecosystem,*" where success grows through shared learning.

Growing Strong

The Kamau Family's Expansion Strategy

Growing too fast can be as dangerous as not growing at all. The Kamau family's agricultural supply store in Nakuru shows us the art of patient expansion. Their rule? Wait for 18 months of solid profits before opening each new location.

"*Many businesses die from growing too fast,*" Mr. Kamau notes. "*We grow like a baobab, slowly but strongly.*" This approach reflects the sustainable growth model taught in business schools but adapted to East African realities.

Your Entrepreneurial Journey Begins

Ready to start your own business story? Begin with these steps:

1. Spend one week observing your community's needs and opportunities
2. Talk to 10 potential customers about their challenges
3. List three ways you could solve these challenges
4. Calculate the minimum resources needed to start
5. Identify potential mentors or business groups in your area

Remember, every business empire started with a single step. Peter Otieno began with two acres. Sarah Mugisha started with a laptop and a dream. The Mwanga family's digital journey began with one mobile money account.

What first step will you take today?

Your business journey isn't just about making money – it's about creating value that can sustain generations. In East Africa's rich soil of opportunity, your entrepreneurial spirit can grow into something amazing. All it needs is your first seed of action.

What problem in your community will you solve? What need will you fill? Your business story begins now.

Cultivating the Wealth Mindset

Objective: To prepare yourself mentally and emotionally for the wealth-building process.

Your mindset shapes your financial future. A wealth mindset is built on principles of abundance, strategic thinking, and perseverance. By shifting your perspective and adopting positive financial habits, you can create lasting success.

Exercise 18: Cultivating the Wealth Mindset

Instructions: Developing a wealth mindset is crucial. This mindset focuses on abundance, long-term vision, and the persistence needed to build wealth over time. Reflect on your current mindset regarding money and wealth, and commit to cultivating a mindset that will help you achieve your goals.

Reflection Questions:

1. How do you currently view money? As a tool, a source of stress, or something else?
2. What can you do to shift from a scarcity mindset to an abundance mindset?

3. How can you maintain a long-term perspective in the face of financial setbacks?

Space for Notes:

Exercise 19: Overcoming Self-Doubt and Fear

Instructions: Fear and self-doubt are common roadblocks in the journey to wealth. Write about any fears or doubts you may have about building wealth. Be honest and acknowledge the emotions that come up.

Reflection Questions:

1. What fears hold you back from pursuing your wealth-building goals?
2. What strategies can you use to overcome these fears and take bold action?

Space for Notes:

9 - Empowering Yourself and Your Family

Picture this: A group of women sitting under an acacia tree in rural Uganda, smartphones in hand, enthusiastically discussing investment strategies while their children play nearby. This isn't a scene from the future,it's happening right now across East Africa, where financial education is transforming lives one family at a time. Welcome to the new face of financial empowerment in East Africa.

The Revolution of Financial Knowledge

"*Money talks, but financial education makes it sing,*" says Mama Agnes, a community leader in Tanzania who transformed her family's fortune through dedicated learning. Like many East Africans, she discovered that financial education isn't just about understanding numbers, it's about unlocking doors to possibilities that span generations.

Think of financial literacy as learning a new language, the language of prosperity. In today's East Africa, this language has evolved beyond the basics of saving and spending. It now encompasses everything from mobile banking to cryptocurrency, from traditional saving circles to modern investment apps.

Starting with Strong Roots: The Art of Budgeting

Remember the old saying about building a house on solid ground? The same applies to your financial future. John Kamau, a teacher in Nairobi-Kenya, laughs when he recalls his early budgeting attempts: "*I used to think budgeting meant simply writing down expenses. Now I know it's about telling your money where to go, instead of wondering where it went!*"

Here's what modern budgeting looks like in East African households:

- **Daily tracking through mobile apps or traditional notebooks**
- **Family budget meetings where even children participate**
- **Zero-based budgeting, where every shilling has a purpose**
- **Regular review and adjustment of spending patterns**

From Saving to Growing: The Strategic Path

"*Saving money is like planting a seed,*" explains Sarah Mutesi, a successful entrepreneur in Rwanda. "*But knowing how to nurture that seed, that's where the magic happens.*" The journey from saving to growing wealth involves several key stages:

Emergency Funds: Your Financial Shield

Think of an emergency fund as your financial umbrella, you might not need it every day, but when it rains, you'll be grateful you have it. Most successful East African families aim to save 3-6 months of living expenses, often starting with just 1,000 shillings a week.

Strategic Saving: Beyond the Basics

Smart saving isn't just about putting money aside, it's about making your money work harder than you do. Consider these popular approaches in East Africa:

- Automatic savings through mobile money platforms
- Goal-specific savings accounts for education, housing, or business

- Rotating savings groups that combine social support with financial discipline

Investment Wisdom: Growing Your Wealth

Smart investing isn't about having a fortune, it's about building one. Whether through savings, partnerships, or innovative funding, East African entrepreneurs are proving that strategic investments can turn small beginnings into lasting success. "*I used to think investing was only for the wealthy*," shares James Okello, a small business owner in Kenya. "*Now I know it's about starting small and being consistent.*"

The Digital Revolution in Financial Education

Technology has become the great equalizer in financial education. Mobile apps now offer:

- Real-time expense tracking
- Investment monitoring
- Financial education courses
- Community support groups

Building Your Family's Financial Legacy

Remember Mama Agnes from earlier? Her story continues through her children. "*My greatest achievement isn't the money I've saved or invested*," she says. "*It's seeing my children teach their friends about compound interest and investment diversification.*"

Creating a family financial legacy involves:

- Regular family discussions about money management

- Practical exercises in budgeting and saving for children
- Shared investment decisions and learning experiences
- Celebration of financial milestones together

The Power of Community Learning

Financial education thrives in community settings. The success of groups like the Tumaini Women's Savings Circle in Tanzania shows how collective learning accelerates personal growth. "*We learn from each other's successes and mistakes*," explains their leader. "*It's like having a hundred financial advisors who are also your friends!*"

Key Action Steps

1. Start your financial education journey today, even if it's just learning one new concept.
2. Share your knowledge with family members, especially children
3. Join or create a community learning group
4. Embrace digital tools while maintaining traditional wisdom
5. Set clear financial goals and celebrate progress along the way

Remember, in the words of Mama Agnes, "*Financial knowledge is the one inheritance that can never be stolen or lost, it only grows as you share it.*"

The path to financial empowerment starts with a single step. Take that step today, and let your journey to financial mastery begin. Your future self, and future generations,will thank you for it.

The Importance of Financial Literacy

Objective: To emphasize the importance of financial literacy as the foundation for wealth creation, and to equip readers with practical tools to improve their financial understanding and decision-making.

Making informed financial choices requires a solid grasp of key concepts like budgeting, saving, credit management, and investing. Strengthening financial literacy not only enhances personal financial well-being but also empowers future generations with valuable knowledge.

Exercise 20: Understanding Your Financial Landscape

Instructions: Begin by assessing your current financial situation. Take an honest inventory of your income, expenses, debts, and assets. This exercise will serve as a baseline for your financial growth and help you understand where you are before you can move forward.

Reflection Questions:

1. What are your main sources of income?
2. What recurring expenses do you have (e.g., rent, utilities, transportation)?
3. What debts do you owe, and how do they impact your cash flow?
4. What assets (e.g., property, savings, investments) do you currently have?

Space for Notes:

Exercise 21: Budgeting Basics, Building a Practical Budget

Instructions: A solid budget is the foundation for financial stability. In this exercise, you will create a practical budget using the income and expenses you identified in the previous exercise. This budget will help you control spending, save more, and allocate funds toward your financial goals.

Steps:

1. List all your monthly sources of income.
2. Categorize your expenses into essentials (e.g., food, housing) and non-essentials (e.g., entertainment, subscriptions).
3. Allocate a portion of your income to savings and investments.
4. Identify areas where you can reduce spending to increase your savings rate.

Reflection Questions:

1. How much of your monthly income is allocated to savings and investments?
2. What spending habits could you adjust to increase your savings rate?
3. Are there any subscriptions or expenses you could eliminate or reduce?

Space for Notes:

Exercise 22: Building an Emergency Fund

Instructions: An emergency fund is a critical aspect of financial literacy and financial security. This fund acts as a safety net during unexpected financial setbacks (e.g., medical expenses, job loss, etc.). Use this exercise to determine how much you need for your emergency fund and how you will achieve that goal.

Steps:

1. Set a target for your emergency fund. Typically, it's recommended to save three to six months' worth of living expenses.
2. Decide how much you can realistically save each month to build this fund.
3. Choose a secure account (e.g., a high-yield savings account) to keep your emergency fund.
4. Track your progress and adjust your budget to prioritize building the fund.

Reflection Questions:

1. How much would you need to cover three to six months of living expenses?
2. How long will it take to save this amount based on your current budget?
3. How can you prioritize savings for your emergency fund?

Space for Notes:

Exercise 23: Understanding and Managing Debt

Instructions: Managing debt is a vital aspect of financial literacy. High levels of debt can significantly undermine your wealth-building efforts. In this exercise, you'll assess your current debt situation and create a plan to manage or pay off your debt strategically.

Steps:

1. List all your debts (e.g., credit card balances, loans, mortgages).
2. Identify the interest rates and minimum payments associated with each debt.
3. Prioritize paying off high-interest debts first (e.g., credit cards) while maintaining minimum payments on others.
4. Consider strategies such as debt snowball (paying off small debts first) or debt avalanche (focusing on high-interest debts).

Reflection Questions:

1. What debts have the highest interest rates, and how can you pay them off more quickly?
2. Are there any debts that you can consolidate or refinance to lower interest rates?
3. How can you avoid accumulating more debt in the future?

Space for Notes:

Exercise 24: Teaching Financial Literacy to Children

Instructions: One of the most powerful gifts you can give future generations is financial literacy. This exercise will help you begin teaching your children or younger family members about the basics of money, budgeting, saving, and investing.

Steps:

1. Choose an age-appropriate method to teach your children about money (e.g., using visual aids for younger kids, online resources for teens).
2. Discuss concepts such as saving for future needs, avoiding debt, and understanding the value of work.
3. Introduce simple saving and investing tools such as piggy banks, savings accounts, or educational apps.

Reflection Questions:

1. How will you introduce the concept of budgeting and saving to your children?
2. What resources (books, videos, games) can you use to make financial literacy fun and engaging?
3. How can you model good financial habits for your children?

Space for Notes:

10 - Risk Management

Imagine building a beautiful house without a roof or foundation, that's what creating wealth without risk management looks like. In East Africa's dynamic landscape, protecting your wealth is just as important as growing it. Let's explore how successful families in our region shield their hard-earned wealth from life's uncertainties.

Understanding Risk: Our East African Reality

"*Risk isn't just about losing money,*" explains David Mutua, a successful business owner in Nairobi-Kenya. "*It's about understanding what could go wrong and preparing for it.*" David learned this lesson when political unrest in 2017 temporarily shut down his business. Today, his thriving enterprise operates across three East African countries, a direct result of the lessons he learned about risk management.

Let's break down the key risks we face in East Africa, using real examples that might feel familiar:

Market Risks: The Ups and Downs

Remember when the Nairobi Securities Exchange dropped 30% in 2020? Smart investors who had spread their investments across different assets, stocks, real estate, and business ventures, weathered that storm better than those who hadn't.

Political Risks: Navigating Change

When Grace Mukasa's transport business faced challenges during Uganda's 2021 elections, her decision to operate across multiple East African countries helped her maintain a stable income. "*Don't put all your eggs in one country's basket,*" she advises with a smile.

Environmental Risks: Nature's Challenge

After losing crops to drought in 2019, Sarah Kioko's family in Kenya now combines farming with urban rental properties. "*Nature is unpredictable,*" she says, "*but having different income sources helps us sleep better at night.*"

Know Yourself: Personal Risk Assessment

Before we dive into protection strategies, let's talk about your personal relationship with risk. Think of it like choosing a vehicle—some people feel comfortable with a sporty car, while others prefer a reliable SUV. Your choice depends on:

- Your current financial situation
- Your family's needs and goals
- Your timeline for wealth-building
- Your emotional comfort with uncertainty

Building Your Protection Shield

Strategy 1: Smart Diversification

The Omondi family in Kenya offers a perfect example of clever diversification:

- Urban rental properties in Nairobi
- Maize farming in Western Kenya
- A transport business serving Uganda and Tanzania
- Investments in government bonds
- Shares in stable regional companies

"*We didn't build this portfolio overnight*," explains Mr. Omondi. "*We started small and expanded gradually, always making sure new investments didn't depend on the same factors as our existing ones.*"

Strategy 2: Insurance as Your Safety Net

Think of insurance as your financial umbrella, you might not need it every day, but when it rains, you'll be grateful you have it. Consider:

- Health insurance to protect against medical emergencies
- Property insurance for your investments
- Crop insurance for agricultural ventures
- Business interruption insurance for your enterprises

The Kagume family in Rwanda learned this lesson the hard way when a fire damaged their warehouse. "*Having proper insurance meant we could rebuild quickly instead of losing everything*," shares Mrs. Kagume.

Strategy 3: Emergency Funds: Your Financial Buffer

Smart wealth builders in East Africa maintain three levels of emergency funds:

1. **Quick Access Fund:** 3-6 months of expenses in easily accessible accounts
2. **Investment Buffer:** 6-12 months of expenses in short-term investments
3. **Opportunity Fund:** Extra savings for unexpected opportunities or major challenges

Technology: Your Risk Management Partner

Today's technology makes risk management easier than ever. Here are tools popular in East Africa:

- M-PESA and similar platforms for quick fund transfers during emergencies
- Pesapal for tracking business expenses and cash flow
- Marketforce for monitoring market trends
- Local bank apps with investment monitoring features
- WhatsApp groups for sharing market intelligence with trusted networks

Community Wisdom in Risk Management

The Arusha Investment Circle provides a fantastic example of community-based risk management. This group of 30 families meets monthly to:

- Share market intelligence
- Pool resources for larger investments
- Provide emergency support to members
- Exchange risk management strategies

"*Our strength comes from shared knowledge*," explains chairperson Maria Sanga. "*When one member faces a challenge, they benefit from the experience of 29 other families*."

Practical Steps for Getting Started

1. Begin with a simple risk assessment of your current wealth
2. Start building your emergency fund, even if it's small
3. Investigate insurance options relevant to your situation
4. Join or create a local investment group

5. Download and learn to use basic financial monitoring apps

Remember that risk management isn't a one-time task. it's an ongoing journey. As your wealth grows, your protection strategies should evolve. The most successful families in East Africa review their risk management strategies at least quarterly, making adjustments as needed.

Key Takeaways

- Start with understanding your personal risk tolerance
- Build protection through diversification, insurance, and emergency funds
- Use technology to monitor and manage risks
- Learn from community wisdom and experiences
- Regularly review and adjust your strategies

As the Swahili proverb says, "*Majuto ni mjukuu*" (Regret is a grandchild). Don't wait for problems to arise, start protecting your wealth today. Your future generations will thank you for the wisdom and foresight you showed in safeguarding their inheritance.

Risk Management: Safeguarding Your Wealth

Objective: To help readers understand the importance of protecting their wealth from risks and uncertainties by employing sound risk management strategies.

Risk management is the process of identifying, assessing, and minimizing potential risks to your wealth. It includes everything from protecting your investments with insurance to diversifying your assets to safeguard against market fluctuations. This chapter offers practical advice for managing the risks that come with wealth-building.

Exercise 25: Identifying Personal and Financial Risks

Instructions: Before you can manage risk, you need to identify where potential threats to your wealth may come from. Take a step back and think about both personal and financial risks you face, and how they might impact your wealth-building goals.

Steps:

1. Make a list of personal risks (e.g., health issues, family emergencies) that could disrupt your financial security.
2. Consider external financial risks such as market fluctuations, business risks, or changes in government policies.
3. Prioritize the risks that could have the most significant impact on your financial goals.

Reflection Questions:

1. How prepared are you to handle unexpected personal or family health issues?
2. What financial risks could derail your investment plans or business ventures?
3. How can you minimize the likelihood of these risks occurring?

Space for Notes:

Exercise 26: Building a Risk Management Plan for Investments

Instructions: One of the most critical aspects of risk management is protecting your investments. This exercise will help you create a plan to protect your financial assets and mitigate risks that may arise.

Steps:

1. Identify the types of investments you currently have, and the risks associated with each.
2. Develop strategies for protecting your investments. This may include using stop-loss orders for stocks, diversifying your portfolio, or buying insurance for physical assets like property.
3. Review your investment portfolio regularly to ensure it remains well-diversified and aligned with your risk tolerance.

Reflection Questions:

1. How can you minimize the risks associated with the investments you hold?
2. Are there any assets in your portfolio that are overexposed to a particular type of risk (e.g., stock market volatility, sector-specific downturn)?
3. How can you ensure that your investments align with your long-term financial goals and risk tolerance?

Space for Notes:

Exercise 27: Understanding and Utilizing Insurance

Instructions: Insurance is a key part of a risk management strategy, as it helps you protect your wealth from unexpected events. In this exercise, you'll explore the different types of insurance and how they can be incorporated into your financial plan.

Steps:

1. Identify the types of insurance you currently have (e.g., life, health, property, auto).
2. Determine if your current coverage is adequate to protect your wealth and assets.
3. Consider additional types of insurance that may be appropriate for your circumstances (e.g., business insurance, liability insurance).
4. Shop around for the best insurance rates and coverage.

Reflection Questions:

1. What types of insurance do you currently have, and how do they protect your assets?
2. Are there any areas where your insurance coverage is lacking?
3. How can you ensure you're getting the best value for your insurance?

Space for Notes:

Exercise 28: Creating a Risk Management Plan for Your Family

Instructions: Just as you create a financial plan, it's important to create a risk management plan for your family. This plan should include strategies for mitigating risks related to health, income loss, and financial instability.

Reflection Questions:

1. What steps can you take to protect your family's financial future (e.g., life insurance, estate planning)?
2. How can you ensure that your family is prepared for financial emergencies?
3. What actions can you take to minimize risks in your business or investments?

Space for Notes:

11 - Legacy Planning: Crafting a Lasting Financial Legacy

What story will your wealth tell when you're gone? Will it speak of wisdom passed down, values preserved, and communities uplifted? Or will it whisper tales of missed opportunities and family discord?

In a small café in Nairobi, James Ndungu leans forward, his eyes bright with purpose. "*Twenty years ago*," he begins, "*my father gathered us all, children, grandchildren, even our closest business partners—and shared his vision for our family's future. That meeting changed everything. Today, our family business doesn't just thrive; it unites* us."

Beyond Money: The Heart of Legacy

Legacy planning in East Africa isn't just about passing down wealth, it's about preserving the soul of your success. When Margaret Okello, a successful retailer in Uganda, began planning her legacy, she realized something profound: "*My children needed to inherit not just my shops, but my shopping wisdom.*"

The Three Pillars of Lasting Legacy

1. **Values First, Valuables Second** "*Before we discussed shillings and securities*," shares Ahmed Hassan, a prominent Tanzanian businessman, "*we documented our family's core values. What do we stand for? What principles guide our decisions? These became our North Star.*"
2. **Knowledge as Currency** "*I taught my children how to count money*," smiles Grace Mutua, a real estate mogul in Kenya, "*but more importantly, I taught them how to make money count for something greater than themselves.*"

3. **Community as Inheritance** The Rwandan proverb says says “*Umwana Urazwe ishyamba aragwa n'ubutwari bwo kuririnda.*" it best: "*A child who inherits a forest must also inherit the responsibility to protect it.*"

Building Your Legacy Blueprint

Start with Heart

Before diving into legal documents and trust structures, gather your family and ask:

- What values define us?
- What impact do we want to have on our community?
- How can our wealth serve future generations?

The Family Constitution

The Ndungu family's success started with their family constitution, which included:

- Core values and principles
- Decision-making processes
- Education requirements for heirs
- Community responsibility guidelines
- Conflict resolution mechanisms

"*It wasn't easy getting everyone to agree*," James Ndungu admits. "*But those difficult conversations prevented even more difficult situations later.*"

Practical Steps in Legacy Building

1. Education as a Foundation

The Okello Family Academy shows how to prepare heirs:

- Monthly financial literacy workshops
- Apprenticeships in family businesses
- Community service requirements
- Regular family council meetings
- Mentorship programs with experienced family members

2. Legal Framework with Cultural Wisdom

Consider how the Kimani family in Kenya balanced tradition with legal protection:

- Created a family trust that respected traditional inheritance customs
- Established clear criteria for leadership succession
- Built-in protection for vulnerable family members
- Incorporated community benefit programs

3. Communication is Key

"*We meet every quarter*," explains Sarah Mugisha from Rwanda. "*Not just to discuss business, but to strengthen bonds. Our family gatherings combine financial updates with storytelling, ensuring our history and values live on.*"

Technology Meets Tradition

Modern tools can strengthen traditional practices:

- Family WhatsApp groups for regular updates
- Digital archives of family history and business documentation
- Online education platforms for next-generation training
- Mobile apps for tracking family investments
- Virtual family council meetings

Managing Emotional Dynamics

"*Money talks*," says Elder Mwangi, a respected family patriarch, "*but emotions shout*." Here's how successful families handle the emotional aspects:

- Regular family retreats for bonding
- Professional mediators for difficult discussions
- Clear communication channels for all family members
- Recognition of both financial and emotional contributions
- Celebration of family milestones and achievements

Community Impact as a Legacy

The Hajji family in Uganda shows how legacy can benefit communities:

- Established scholarship programs
- Created business incubation centers
- Built community health facilities
- Supported local environmental initiatives

"*Our greatest legacy*," says Hajji Ibrahim, "*is the smiles we put on faces we may never see*."

Common Pitfalls and Solutions

Challenge: Unequal Business Aptitude

Solution: The Mahmoud family created different roles for different strengths, some children manage investments, and others handle community programs.

Challenge: Traditional vs. Modern Expectations

Solution: The Okonjo family developed a hybrid system that honors traditional inheritance practices while ensuring business continuity.

Your Legacy Journey Starts Now

Remember:

1. Start with values and vision
2. Build strong communication channels
3. Invest in next-generation education
4. Balance tradition with modern tools
5. Include community impact
6. Plan for emotional as well as financial aspects

Final Thoughts

As we say in Swahili, "*Mtoto umleavyo ndivyo akuavyo*" (A child grows according to how they are raised). Your legacy is growing right now, with every decision you make and every value you demonstrate.

Legacy Planning: Crafting a Lasting Financial Legacy

Objective: To introduce the concept of legacy planning, emphasizing how to build wealth that endures for generations. Legacy planning is about more than just passing on assets, it's about instilling values, providing financial literacy, and ensuring long-term family prosperity.

A strong financial legacy is more than just passing down assets, it's about ensuring future generations are equipped with financial knowledge, shared values, and a vision for long-term prosperity. Thoughtful legacy planning includes structuring wealth distribution, fostering financial responsibility, and preparing heirs to manage and grow inherited wealth.

Exercise 29: Creating a Family Mission Statement

Instructions: A family mission statement is a powerful tool that aligns family values with wealth-building goals. This exercise will help you create a mission statement that reflects your family's aspirations for the future.

Steps:

1. Gather your family members and discuss your shared values, financial goals, and long-term aspirations.
2. Identify the core values you want to instill in future generations (e.g., integrity, education, financial responsibility).
3. Craft a concise mission statement that reflects these values and outlines your family's vision for financial success and legacy.

4. Ensure that everyone in your family understands and is aligned with the mission statement.

Reflection Questions:

1. What values are most important to your family, and how do they influence your financial goals?
2. How can you use your family mission statement to guide wealth-building decisions?
3. What steps can you take to ensure that future generations uphold the mission and values outlined in the statement?

4. **Space for Notes**:

Exercise 30: Establishing a Trust Fund or Estate Plan

Instructions: Establishing a trust or creating an estate plan is a key step in protecting your wealth and ensuring it's passed down effectively. In this exercise, you'll explore how to set up a trust or will that outlines how your wealth will be distributed among your heirs.

Steps:

1. Consult with a legal or financial expert to discuss your options for estate planning (e.g., creating a will, setting up a trust fund).
2. Outline your wishes for how assets should be distributed, including property, investments, and family businesses.
3. Consider creating a living trust to avoid probate and ensure a smooth transition of wealth.
4. Review your estate plan regularly to reflect any changes in your family or financial situation.

Reflection Questions:

1. What are your top priorities when it comes to distributing your wealth to future generations?
2. How will you ensure that your estate plan is clear and legally binding?
3. Who will be responsible for managing your estate after your passing, and how will they ensure that your wishes are carried out?

Space for Notes:

Exercise 31: Family Legacy Vision Board

Instructions: A vision board helps visualize your goals, and in this case, it will serve as a visual representation of your family's financial and personal legacy. This exercise helps you clarify and focus on the type of legacy you want to leave.

Steps:

1. Gather magazines, printouts, or digital images of your vision for your family's future (e.g., educational opportunities, wealth, health, and happiness).
2. Create a vision board that reflects the financial and personal legacy you want to leave behind. Include images of things like:
   - Your children's education

    - Real estate investments
    - Family business successes
    - Community service or philanthropy
3. Display your vision board in a place where you and your family can see it regularly.

Reflection Questions:

1. What legacy do you want to leave behind for your family?
2. How can your vision board help guide your financial decisions?
3. How will you involve your children or family members in carrying on your legacy?

Space for Notes:

Exercise 32: Creating a Family Legacy Trust

Instructions: Establishing a family trust is an essential component of legacy planning. This exercise will guide you through the process of setting up a trust that ensures your wealth is passed down efficiently and according to your wishes.

Steps:

1. **Consult a Legal Expert**: Work with a lawyer or financial advisor to discuss the specifics of creating a family trust.
2. **Define Trust Terms**: Decide what assets will be placed in the trust and how they should be distributed among family members.
3. **Assign Trustees**: Appoint a trusted person or a group to manage the trust after you pass.
4. **Review Regularly**: Periodically review your trust to ensure it still aligns with your goals.

Reflection Questions:

1. What assets do you want to include in your trust, and why?
2. Who will be responsible for managing the trust after your passing?
3. How can you ensure that the trust's terms reflect your family's values and needs?

Space for Notes:

12 - Embracing Technology in Wealth Creation

"*I used to walk four hours to the nearest bank*," says Sarah Kemunto, her eyes twinkling as she pulls out her smartphone. "*Now my bank fits in my pocket.*" With a few taps, she shows me how she manages her shop's inventory, processes customer payments, and invests in government securities, all from a device that costs less than a mo00000nth's profit from her small grocery store in rural Kenya.

The Digital Revolution at Your Fingertips

East Africa isn't just adopting digital finance, we're reinventing it. Recent data from the World Bank (2023) shows our region leading the continent in mobile money adoption:

- **Kenya:** 84% of adults use mobile money services.
- **Tanzania:** 77% of adults are digitally connected.
- **Uganda:** 70% of the population engaged in digital transactions
- **Rwanda:** 76% of adults use digital financial services.

Beyond M-Pesa: The New Financial Frontier

"*When M-Pesa, came, we thought it was just for sending money home*," chuckles James Omondi, a successful retailer in Nairobi-Kenay. "*Today, it's the backbone of my business empire.*" The numbers tell the story: mobile money users in East Africa conducted transactions worth $490 billion in 2022 (East African Business Council Report, 2023), representing a 47% increase from 2021.

Real Stories, Real Transformation

The Shop That Technology Built

Meet Grace Muteshi, whose tiny roadside shop in Nakuru, Kenya, became a thriving mini-market chain. Her story exemplifies the regional trend: small businesses using digital tools saw an average revenue increase of 35% in their first year of adoption (Digital Business Report, 2023).

Today, Grace manages five stores through her smartphone, using:

- Digital inventory management
- Mobile payment systems
- Customer loyalty apps
- Data analytics for business decisions

The Digital Toolkit for Wealth Creation

Mobile Money: Your Financial Command Center

According to the 2023 East African Fintech Report, the modern mobile money ecosystem now includes:

- Instant payments and transfers (98% completion rate)
- Savings accounts with up to 7% annual interest
- Micro-loans (average processing time: 3 minutes)
- Bill payments and merchant services
- Investment opportunities starting from $1

Investment Apps: Wall Street in Your Pocket

The democratization of investment has arrived. Regional investment platforms report:

- 300% growth in retail investors (2021-2023)
- Average starting investment: $5-10
- Most popular: Government securities and mutual funds
- 65% of users are under 35 years old

Digital Education: Learning Without Limits

"*Knowledge used to be for those who could afford expensive seminars*," says Teacher Mary from Uganda. "*Now my students learn financial literacy from free apps and YouTube videos*." In 2023, over 2 million East Africans accessed online financial education resources, with a 200% increase in local language content.

Popular Learning Platforms

Regional statistics show the most effective platforms offer:

- Multi-language support (7+ local languages)
- Gamified learning experiences
- Community features
- Progress tracking

The E-Commerce Evolution

The digital marketplace transformation is remarkable. From 2020 to 2023:

- Online businesses grew by 156%
- Mobile payments for online purchases increased by 287%
- Cross-border e-commerce expanded by 94%

Emmanuel Bahati's journey from market vendor to e-commerce success exemplifies this trend. "*Social media turned my market stall into an international business*," he beams. His story reflects the broader regional shift: 67% of small businesses now have some form of digital presence.

Protecting Your Digital Wealth

"*Technology is like fire*," warns cybersecurity expert Amina Hassan. Regional data shows:

- 45% reduction in fraud cases where two-factor authentication is used.
- 78% of security breaches involve weak passwords.
- Community-based security awareness programs show 89% effectiveness.

The Community Goes Digital

Traditional saving circles (*chamas*) have evolved dramatically. The Upendo Digital Chama's success shows why:

- 300+ members managing $2.5M in assets
- 98% meeting attendance through virtual platforms
- 45% higher returns compared to traditional chamas

Bridging the Digital Divide

David Mukasa's Digital Villages Initiative demonstrates the power of community-based tech adoption:

- 5,000 rural residents trained
- 20 community tech hubs established
- 85% participant retention rate

- 67% female participation

The Future is Here: Emerging Technologies

East Africa is pioneering several technological innovations:

- Blockchain land registry pilots showing 90% reduction in disputes
- AI-powered credit scoring increasing loan approval rates by 60%
- Digital currency projects reducing cross-border transaction costs by 70%

Your Digital Journey Starts Now

1. **Start small:** Download a mobile money app.
2. **Learn continuously:** Join online financial communities.
3. **Experiment safely:** Try investment apps with small amounts.
4. **Share knowledge:** Teach others in your community.
5. **Stay secure:** Practice digital safety.

The digital revolution in East Africa isn't just changing how we handle money, it's transforming our entire approach to wealth creation. As Sarah Kemunto says, "*Yesterday's impossibilities are today's opportunities.*"

Your smartphone isn't just a phone, it's your gateway to financial freedom. The future of wealth creation is digital, and it's already here in East Africa. The only question is: how will you write your digital success story?

Embracing Technology in Wealth Creation

Objective: To explore how digital innovations are reshaping wealth-building strategies and provide practical guidance on integrating technology into financial planning, investment, and economic growth.

Exercise 33: Exploring Digital Financial Tools

Instructions: In today's digital world, leveraging technology is essential for staying ahead in financial management and wealth creation. This exercise will guide you through identifying and exploring digital tools that can help you manage your finances, invest smartly, and track your financial progress.

Steps:

1. **Research Tools**: Identify digital tools that could assist with your personal or family finances. Look for tools that cover budgeting, savings, investment tracking, and even mobile payments. A few examples include:
   - **Budgeting tools** (e.g., Mint, YNAB, or local options like PesaPal)
   - **Mobile banking apps** (e.g., M-Pesa, MTN and Airtel Money)
   - **Investment platforms** (e.g., Bamboo, Cowrywise, or other fintech services in East Africa)
2. **Evaluate Features**: For each tool you find, evaluate its features. Is it user-friendly? Does it allow you to set goals? Does it provide real-time updates on your spending or investments?

3. **Set Up Accounts**: If you haven't already, create accounts with these tools. Start small, link your bank account, set up your monthly budget, or start tracking your investments.
4. **Track Your Progress**: Begin using these tools consistently for at least 30 days. Keep track of any improvements in your financial awareness or the ease with which you manage your wealth.

Reflection Questions:

1. How easy was it to navigate and use these digital tools?
2. What insights have you gained from using these tools for the first time?
3. How will you integrate these tools into your daily financial routine moving forward?

Space for Notes:

Exercise 34: Implementing E-commerce in Your Wealth Strategy

Instructions: With the rise of online business and digital platforms, e-commerce has become a significant avenue for wealth generation. This exercise will help you explore how you can use e-commerce or online businesses to diversify your income streams.

Steps:

1. **Identify Market Gaps**: Research the e-commerce space in your region. What products or services are in demand? Are there local artisans, farmers, or entrepreneurs who could benefit from online exposure? Is there a niche market that you can serve?
2. **Develop a Business Idea**: Based on your findings, create an e-commerce business idea. It could be:
    - Selling locally made products online (e.g., crafts, food items, clothing)
    - Starting a service-based business (e.g., freelance writing, design, online tutoring)
    - Dropshipping or reselling products
3. **Choose a Platform**: Decide where to host your business. This could be on an existing platform (e.g., Jumia, Etsy, or Shopify) or creating your own website. Take note of the costs and features of these platforms, as well as any limitations.
4. **Marketing Your E-commerce Business**: Create a marketing plan to promote your business. Will you use social media, influencer marketing, or search engine optimization (SEO)? Think about your target audience and how best to reach them.

Reflection Questions:

1. What challenges do you anticipate when setting up an e-commerce business?
2. How can you use your community network to market your online business?
3. What digital tools can you use to streamline the operation of your online business (e.g., payment gateways, logistics)?

Space for Notes:

Exercise 35: Exploring Digital Payment Solutions

Instructions: In many parts of East Africa, mobile money services such as M-Pesa,MTN & Airtel Money, and others have revolutionized financial transactions. This exercise will help you understand how to use digital payment systems to streamline your financial processes and enhance your wealth-building efforts.

Steps:

1. **Research Available Services**: Identify at least three mobile payment platforms that are widely used in your region. These could include M-Pesa,MTN,Airtel Money, Tigo Pesa, or international platforms like PayPal or Google Pay.
2. **Sign Up for a Service**: Choose one platform to sign up for, if you haven't already. Learn how to transfer money, pay bills, and use the service for personal or business transactions.
3. **Evaluate Benefits**: Think about how this platform can improve your financial life. For example, will it make it easier to save, transfer funds, or access credit?
4. **Experiment with Features**: Start by using the platform for small transactions. As you become familiar with the service, try using it to pay bills, transfer funds to family members, or even save a small amount regularly.

Reflection Questions:

1. What did you learn about mobile payments that you didn't know before?
2. How might digital payment systems help you manage your personal or business finances more efficiently?

3. What new opportunities for wealth-building might digital payment services unlock for you?

Space for Notes:

Exercise 36: Investing in Digital Assets

Instructions: The digital economy has opened up new ways to invest and build wealth, including through cryptocurrency, digital real estate, and e-commerce. This exercise will guide you in exploring digital assets as a potential component of your investment strategy.

Steps:

1. **Research Cryptocurrency**: Learn about popular cryptocurrencies like Bitcoin, Ethereum, and local alternatives. Find out how they work, the risks involved, and how people are using them for investments.
2. **Explore Digital Real Estate**: Consider virtual real estate in digital spaces like Decentraland or The Sandbox. Research how people are buying, selling, and renting virtual properties as part of a broader digital investment strategy.
3. **Evaluate E-commerce Investments**: Explore how platforms like Amazon, eBay, or Shopify offer opportunities for digital entrepreneurship. Are there products or services you can sell or invest in online?
4. **Create a Digital Investment Plan**: Based on your research, create a basic plan for incorporating digital assets into your investment strategy. Start small, and think about the types of risks you're comfortable taking.

Reflection Questions:

1. Do you feel comfortable with the volatility and risks of digital assets like cryptocurrency?
2. What digital investments might be most suitable for you based on your financial goals and risk tolerance?

3. How can digital assets complement your existing investment strategy?

Space for Notes:

13 - Wealth in Unity: How Collective Action Creates Prosperity

"*Kidogo kidogo hujaza kibaba*", Little by little fills the measure. East African Proverb

Picture this: It's early morning in rural Kenya, and under a sprawling acacia tree, ten women gather for what seems like a simple meeting. But this isn't just any meeting, it's the weekly gathering of the Umoja Stokvel, a group that would transform not just their own lives, but their entire community's future.

The Power of Collective Action: By the Numbers

Research from the World Bank's 2023 Community Finance Report reveals the stunning impact of collective wealth building:

- Community savings groups in East Africa manage over $1.2 billion in assets.
- Members of organized savings groups are 3.5 times more likely to start successful businesses.
- Group-based microfinance shows 89% higher repayment rates than individual loans.
- Community investment groups report 47% higher returns than individual investors.

"*When we started, all we had was trust and hope,*" recalls Mama Sarah, one of the founding members of Umoja Stokvel, her eyes sparkling with pride. "*Today, we own the largest community farm in our district. But the real harvest isn't in our fields—it's in the bonds we've built.*"

The Magic of Collective Dreams: Evidence-Based Success

The Journal of African Economies (2023) documents how community wealth-building transforms lives:

- 76% of community group members achieve their financial goals.
- Child education rates increase by 42% in families involved in savings groups.
- Business survival rates are 2.3 times higher with community support.
- Healthcare access improves by 58% for group members.

The Umoja Story: From Small Seeds to Mighty Trees

Let's return to the Umoja Stokvel, whose journey exemplifies these statistics:

2019: Ten women start contributing 500 shillings each monthly

2020: Group expands to 25 members, starts microloans (92% repayment rate)

2021: Purchase the first acre of community land

2022: Launch commercial farming operation (165% ROI)

2023: Employ 50 community members

Today: Own 20 acres, run agricultural training program (trained 300+ farmers)

Modern Tribes, Timeless Wisdom

According to the African Development Bank's 2023 report on Financial Inclusion:

- Digital community savings platforms have shown 234% growth since 2020.
- 67% of successful community groups use hybrid meeting models.
- Mobile money integration increases participation by 156%.
- Technology-enabled groups show 43% higher retention rates.

Meet the Digital Chama Champions of Kampala-Uganda: "*We use WhatsApp for daily communication, mobile money for contributions, and cloud accounting for transparency*," explains Samuel, the group's coordinator. Their success metrics:

- 98%-member retention rate
- 45% higher returns than traditional groups
- 100% digital payment adoption
- Zero cases of financial mismanagement

Beyond Borders: The Global Village

The Harvard Business Review's 2023 study on Collective Economics found that community wealth principles transcend cultures:

- Similar models succeed in 47 countries
- Cross-cultural adaptations show 82% success rates
- Community investment groups outperform individual investors by 34%
- Social capital increases business success rates by 2.7 times

Dr. Angela Martinez, a leading researcher at the Global Community Finance Institute, notes: "*Our five-year study across 15 countries shows that collective wealth-building principles are universal. The ROI on social capital averages 156% when measured in economic outcomes.*"

Building Your Wealth Community: Research-Backed Steps

The African Journal of Economics and Management (2023) identifies key success factors:

1. Start with Trust (Success rate: 94%)
- Begin with 5-15 core members
- Establish written guidelines
- Create transparent tracking systems
- Hold regular accountability meetings
2. Grow with Purpose (Growth multiplier: 3.2x)
- Set SMART collective goals
- Implement structured education programs
- Diversify skills within the group
- Document and celebrate milestones
3. Scale with Wisdom (Sustainability rate: 87%)
- Follow proven expansion models
- Invest in digital infrastructure
- Maintain high-touch relationships
- Create knowledge-sharing systems

Leadership That Serves

Research from the East African Leadership Institute (2023) shows effective community wealth leaders achieve:

- 67% higher group retention rates

- 89% successful project completion
- 123% higher member satisfaction
- 45% better conflict resolution

The Future of Community Wealth

The World Economic Forum's 2023 report on Community Economics projects:

- 300% growth in community wealth initiatives by 2030
- Digital integration increases efficiency by 67%
- Cross-border collaboration growing by 156%
- Youth participation rising by 234%

The Next Generation

Community wealth building isn't just about today—it's about tomorrow. The Youth Enterprise Club in Kampala shows how:

- Mentorship programs pairing experienced investors with youth
- Technology training for modern financial management
- Internship opportunities within member businesses
- Seed funding for youth business initiatives

Your Role in the Story

MIT's Collective Economics Lab (2023) identifies five key success factors:

1. Active participation increases success by 234%
2. Regular knowledge sharing improves outcomes by 167%
3. Structured mentorship boosts results by 189%
4. Technology adoption accelerates growth by 145%

5. Community reinvestment multiplies impact by 278%

The Power of Many: Proven Results

The African Development Bank's 10-year study shows:

- Community wealth groups achieve 3.4x better outcomes
- Social support increases resilience by 256%
- Collective decision-making improves investment returns by 67%
- Intergenerational wealth transfer succeeds 89% more often

Overcoming Common Challenges

Successful community wealth-building groups often face these challenges:

1. Trust Issues

Solution: Regular financial audits and transparent digital tracking

2. Member Commitment

Solution: Clear attendance policies and commitment agreements

3. Investment Decisions

Solution: Established voting procedures and investment criteria

4. Knowledge Gaps

Solution: Regular financial literacy workshops and mentoring programs

Remember Mama Sarah's words: "*When we dream alone, it's just a dream. When we dream together, it's the beginning of reality.*" Now backed by research that collective dreams are 3.7 times more likely to become reality.

Ready to start your community wealth journey? The evidence is clear: together, we grow stronger, smarter, and wealthier.

The Power of Community in Wealth Building

Objective: To highlight the impact of collective financial efforts and provide strategies for leveraging community resources, skills, and networks to build sustainable wealth.

Exercise 37: Assessing Your Community's Resources

Instructions: Take a moment to evaluate the community you are a part of. A strong community is built on shared values and collective resources. This exercise will help you identify how your community's resources can be leveraged for mutual financial success.

Steps:

1. Identify the key strengths of your community (e.g., skills, financial resources, businesses, local leadership).
2. Determine any existing networks or groups that you can join or contribute to (e.g., savings groups, investment clubs, cooperatives).
3. List any businesses or entrepreneurs within your community who could benefit from your support or collaboration.

Reflection Questions:

1. What skills or resources do you personally bring to your community?
2. How can you contribute to or benefit from existing community networks?
3. What collective goals could you work on with your community to create lasting wealth?

Space for Notes:

Exercise 38: Building a Collaborative Wealth Project

Instructions: One of the most effective ways to build wealth together is through collaborative projects. Whether it's pooling funds for a local investment or starting a community business, working together can lead to greater returns. In this exercise, you'll map out a potential community wealth-building project.

Steps:

1. Identify a potential collaborative project in your community (e.g., a real estate development, a local business, or an agricultural initiative).
2. Define the goals and purpose of the project (e.g., wealth generation, employment creation, community development).
3. Assess the resources required for the project (e.g., financial investment, time, skills, infrastructure).
4. Identify the people or groups who could be involved in the project (e.g., local businesses, individuals with expertise).
5. Determine the structure of the project (e.g., partnership, cooperative, community fund).

Reflection Questions:

1. How will the project contribute to the collective wealth of your community?
2. What challenges might arise in starting a community project, and how can you overcome them?
3. What are the expected benefits for participants and the community as a whole?

Space for Notes:

Exercise 39: Overcoming Barriers to Community Wealth

Instructions: Building wealth together often involves overcoming significant cultural, social, and economic barriers. This exercise will help you assess the barriers within your community and come up with practical strategies to overcome them.

Steps:

1. Identify the common barriers that might prevent wealth-building in your community (e.g., lack of trust, unequal access to resources, cultural norms that prevent collective investment).
2. Develop stratcgics to address each barrier (e.g., building trust through transparency, educating the community on the benefits of collective wealth, providing financial literacy programs).

3. Create a plan for initiating conversations with community members to discuss these barriers and propose solutions.

Reflection Questions:

1. What is the most significant barrier to community wealth-building in your area?
2. How can you help educate others about the benefits of pooling resources for mutual success?
3. What steps can you take to increase the community's trust in shared projects or ventures?

Space for Notes:

Exercise 40: Leveraging Technology for Community Empowerment

Instructions: Technology is a powerful tool for transforming community wealth-building efforts. From mobile banking to crowdfunding platforms, technology can expand access to resources and create new opportunities. This exercise will explore how you can leverage technology to support communal wealth projects.

Steps:

1. Research technological tools that could help facilitate community wealth-building (e.g., mobile money platforms, crowdfunding websites, financial apps).
2. Identify the most suitable technology for your community's needs. For example, if your community has limited access to banks, mobile money services like M-Pesa might be ideal.
3. Discuss how technology can be used to streamline financial transactions, provide transparent accounting, and foster collaboration among community members.
4. Develop a strategy for introducing and integrating these technological tools into your community.

Reflection Questions:

1. What technological resources are available to your community, and how can they be better utilized?
2. How can technology reduce barriers to participation in wealth-building initiatives?
3. What tools could help ensure the transparency and security of community investments?

Space for Notes:

Exercise 41: Building a Community Wealth Plan

Instructions: The strength of a community lies in the collective efforts of its members. This exercise will help you create a detailed plan for leveraging community resources to build wealth together.

Steps:

1. **Identify Your Community**: Start by identifying the community you want to focus on. This could be your immediate family, extended family, local neighborhood, or even a broader social network (e.g., an online community of entrepreneurs or investors).
2. **Assess Available Resources**: Look at the assets and talents that members of your community bring. This can include physical resources like land, financial capital, or business

ideas, as well as human resources like skills, expertise, or labor.

3. **Set Collective Goals**: What does your community want to achieve together? Goals could range from starting a joint business, investing in real estate, or even a collective savings or lending fund. Be specific about what success looks like.
4. **Create a Collaborative Action Plan**: Work with the members of your community to define the steps needed to achieve the collective goals. This might include gathering initial investments, launching a business, or identifying funding sources.
5. **Establish Governance and Accountability**: Determine how decisions will be made within the group. Will there be regular meetings? How will profits or assets be distributed? Consider establishing roles and responsibilities for each member.

Reflection Questions:

1. How can you leverage the strengths of your community to achieve your financial goals?
2. What challenges do you anticipate in building wealth together with others?
3. How can you encourage active participation and accountability within your community?

Space for Notes:

Exercise 42: Celebrating Community Successes

Instructions: Acknowledge and celebrate the success of your community efforts, as this creates momentum and reinforces the value of working together. This exercise will help you reflect on your community's achievements and plan for further successes.

Steps:

1. **Review Your Achievements**: Look back at the collective goals your community has achieved so far. What tangible successes have you experienced? Did you start a business, fund a shared investment, or achieve another goal?
2. **Plan a Celebration**: Organize a small event, either in person or virtually, to celebrate the success of your

community. This could be a meeting to discuss your progress, a social gathering, or even a formal event depending on the size of your community.

3. **Reflect and Share Stories**: During the celebration, encourage everyone to share their experiences. What challenges did they overcome? How did collaboration benefit them personally?
4. **Set New Goals**: As you celebrate past success, think about the next steps. What new goals can your community set to continue building wealth together?

Reflection Questions:

1. How did working with a community enrich your personal wealth-building experience?
2. What role does celebration play in sustaining motivation within your community?
3. How can you continue to support each other in achieving future financial goals?

Space for Notes:

Exercise 43: Identifying Potential Community Wealth Projects

Instructions: Building wealth as a community requires identifying projects where resources, skills, and knowledge can be pooled for mutual benefit. In this exercise, you will brainstorm and identify community-based wealth-building initiatives.

Steps:

1. **Brainstorm Ideas**: Think of at least three possible wealth-building projects that could be initiated within your community. These could include:
    - Establishing a cooperative farming project
    - Starting a community-owned business or retail outlet
    - Creating a community investment fund or savings group
2. **Assess Resources**: For each idea, list the resources you need to start the project. Consider funding, skills, community participation, and physical resources (e.g., land, equipment).
3. **Collaborative Planning**: Form a planning team within your community. This team will help in the project's design and launch. Invite local leaders, skilled workers, and entrepreneurs to join forces.
4. **Implementation Plan**: Develop a step-by-step implementation plan for the project, with clear milestones and deadlines. Assign roles and responsibilities to each participant.

Reflection Questions:

1. Which of the ideas excites you the most, and why?
2. What resources are you currently missing to get started?

3. How will you motivate your community to participate in this project?

Space for Notes:

Exercise 44: Setting Up a Community Investment Fund

Instructions: A community investment fund is a pool of resources gathered from community members, often for joint investments. This exercise helps you design and implement a fund that can be used for communal ventures such as real estate, agriculture, or small businesses.

Steps:

1. **Create a Fund Structure**: Decide how the fund will operate. Will it be voluntary, or will there be a fixed contribution requirement? Will it focus on a single project or multiple investments?
2. **Determine Investment Goals**: Define the fund's purpose—are you aiming to generate long-term returns, or are there shorter-term financial goals for the community?
3. **Establish Governance**: Identify how decisions will be made within the group. Who will manage the fund? Will there be regular meetings or a formal committee?
4. **Promote Fund Membership**: Encourage community members to join the fund. Outline the benefits of pooling resources and investing together.
5. **Select Initial Investments**: Use the fund to invest in the community's first project, whether it's buying land, starting a business, or launching a joint venture.

Reflection Questions:

1. What are the potential challenges of starting a community investment fund?
2. How will you ensure transparency and fairness in managing the fund?
3. How will you encourage community members to invest their resources?

Space for Notes:

Conclusion

As we near the end of our journey through *Building Generational Wealth in East African Families*, it's time to pause and reflect on the key themes and practical strategies we've explored. This book has been crafted with a deep understanding of the unique challenges and opportunities East African families face in their pursuit of financial stability and growth. Our goal has been to provide a roadmap tailored to this context, one that recognizes the importance of culture, community, and collaboration in wealth-building.

Throughout these chapters, we've seen that creating generational wealth is not an isolated endeavor. The power of community is at the heart of sustainable financial success. Whether it's pooling resources, sharing knowledge, or offering emotional support, communities have an unmatched ability to amplify individual efforts. Together, we can overcome challenges, seize opportunities, and build wealth that lasts for generations.

As you continue your own journey toward financial prosperity, remember: you don't have to do it alone. Embrace the power of community. Tap into your networks, collaborate with others, and work toward common goals. By doing so, you'll not only elevate your own financial future, but you'll also contribute to a broader movement that uplifts families and communities across East Africa and beyond. The future of wealth in our region depends on our ability to come together, share resources and knowledge, and create legacies that endure for generations to come.

Key Takeaways

1. **The Importance of Mindset**: Developing a wealth-oriented mindset is crucial for long-term financial success. Embracing a perspective that prioritizes growth, resilience, and community can pave the way for transformative changes.
2. **Entrepreneurship and Innovation**: We've examined the significance of entrepreneurship as a pathway to financial independence. By starting and nurturing local businesses, families can create sustainable income sources and contribute to their communities.
3. **Smart Investment Strategies**: From real estate to agriculture and stocks, investing wisely is foundational for building wealth. Understanding local markets and leveraging available resources can lead to fruitful investment opportunities.
4. **Financial Education**: Knowledge is power. Practical financial education modules provide the tools needed for

effective budgeting, understanding credit, and navigating investments, ensuring that families are well-equipped to make informed decisions.

5. **Harnessing Informal Economies**: The potential of informal savings groups, such as stokvels and SACCOs, cannot be overlooked. Integrating these communal systems into formal financial planning can enhance wealth-building efforts and provide stability.
6. **Risk Management**: Learning to assess and manage risks is vital for navigating uncertainties, particularly in fluctuating markets and politically volatile environments. Building a toolkit for risk management empowers families to protect their assets.
7. **Community Support**: The role of community in wealth creation is profound. By pooling resources, sharing knowledge, and supporting one another, families can amplify their wealth-building efforts and create lasting impact.
8. **Legacy Planning**: Establishing a legacy is about more than just financial wealth; it's about values, traditions, and the ethical transfer of assets to future generations. Comprehensive planning ensures that wealth is preserved and passed down effectively.
9. **Embracing Technology**: In an increasingly digital world, leveraging technology can enhance financial management and investment strategies, making wealth-building more accessible.

Moving Forward

As you close this book, remember: the journey to building generational wealth is just beginning. Each chapter has provided valuable tools and insights, but the real transformation happens when you apply these lessons in your own life and community. Knowledge alone is not enough, true change happens through action. Engage with your neighbours, collaborate with local organizations, and spark conversations that promote financial literacy and collective growth.

Let this book be more than just a guide, it should be the starting point for you and your family, the catalyst for meaningful discussions about wealth, legacy, and the future you want to build. Together, we hold the power to rewrite East Africa's financial future, one step, one decision, and one generation at a time.

Thank you for embarking on this journey with me. As you move forward, may your path toward financial prosperity be guided by knowledge, community, and a relentless commitment to building a legacy that stands the test of time.

Acknowledgments

First and foremost, I would like to honor the memory of my late mother, Sande Robina Kakura. Her unwavering faith, love, and prayers were a constant source of strength throughout my life. Even though we were miles apart, she never missed a day without praying for me. I will forever cherish the calls we shared, her determination to FaceTime me every day or weekend, no matter her day's toils and commitment. Her tenacity and dedication to me, even when it meant forcing my older siblings to buy her airtime to keep in touch, will always stay with me. She was, without a doubt, the bravest person I have ever known. This book is as much hers as it is mine, and I dedicate it to her memory.

To my siblings, thank you for your support, in all its forms, as I made the difficult decision to move to Canada. Some of you were excited for me, others not so much, but all of you, in your own way, helped me become who I am today. I have missed so many family celebrations, birthdays, holidays, and gatherings, but know that you've always been in my heart, even if I couldn't be there in person.

To my extended family, your encouragement, love, and understanding have been invaluable. I am grateful for all the ways you've supported me, both emotionally and practically, from afar.

To my dear friend, Emma, thank you for being the one who brought me to Canada. Your belief in me and your willingness to help me adjust to life here has meant the world. Your friendship continues to be a gift in my life; one I will always treasure.

A special thank you goes to Dr. Bielu O.A., a friend and mentor who has been with me every step of the way on this journey. You encouraged me to keep going with my dream of writing, sometimes even helping me with editing and refining my work. Your support has been immeasurable, and you've truly become a coach and confidant, always reminding me to stay focused on my vision. You have helped shape this book in ways words can't fully capture, and I'm forever grateful.

To my nieces, Viola Abigaba, Belinda Twesigye, Claire Babirye, Natasha Umwiza, and the late Melissa Mugisha, thank you for your help in reviewing the transcript and organizing the material. Melissa, my dear daughter, you were there through it all. You not only helped me with reading, revising, and providing advice, but you also contributed to the book's cover design. Though you were taken from us far too soon, I feel your presence with me as this book finally reaches publication. Melissa, I know you will be looking down from heaven, proud of the work we've done together. We did it, my love, and I dedicate this book to you as well. Rest in peace, my dear daughter.

Finally, to everyone who has supported me, believed in me, and helped me through the highs and lows—thank you. This book is a culmination of all the love, encouragement, and strength I have received over the years. I am deeply grateful to each of you.

References:

1. Book: Kimani, M. W. (2018). Financial Literacy and Wealth Building in East African Families. Nairobi Publishers.
2. Book: Gikandi, J. N. (2019). Building Generational Wealth in East Africa: Strategies for Success. East African Publishers.
3. Report: Odundo, J. (2021). Wealth Creation in East African Communities: Case Studies and Best Practices. East African Economic Research Institute.
4. Academic Paper: Kamau, W., & Mwangi, P. (2020). Cultural Factors and Generational Wealth Creation in East Africa. Journal of African Studies, 10(2), 78-95.
5. Book: Kimani, M. W. (2018). Financial Literacy and Wealth Building in East African Families. Nairobi Publishers.
6. Report: East African Development Bank. (2022). Fostering Generational Wealth: Government Policies and Support in East Africa. EADB Publications.
7. Article in a Journal: Forbes. (2023, February 15). 5 Methods For Thriving At Building Black Generational Wealth. Forbes. https://www.forbes.com/sites/forbeseq/2023/02/15/5-methods-for-thriving-at-building-black-generational-wealth/?sh=4640790720ab

End

www.ingramcontent.com/pod-product-compliance
Lightning Source LLC
Chambersburg PA
CBHW031154020426
42333CB00013B/668
* 9 7 8 1 0 6 8 8 7 4 6 0 4 *